HORS D'OEUVRES EVERYBODY LOVES

Party Menus with Recipes to Win Your Heart

Page 19 - Linda's Sombrero Dip
    ✓   9 - Celebration Chili Dip
    ✓   14 - Lemon Squares
    ✓   38 - Brunch Bites
    ✓   39 - Spinach Dip

Hors D'Oeuvres Everybody Loves

PARTY MENUS WITH RECIPES
TO WIN YOUR HEART

by Mary Leigh Furrh
and Jo Barksdale

QUAIL RIDGE PRESS

Dedicated with love to our best tasters—our families—
Mary Leigh's husband, Jim, and children,
Brooke, Shelley, Roy and Leigh,
and Jo's children, Mary, Bethany, Jayne,
Emily and Katherine

Copyright © 1983 by
QUAIL RIDGE PRESS, INC.
First printing, September 1983
Second printing, February 1984
Third printing, April 1987
Fourth printing, July 1989
ISBN 0-937552-11-9
Manufactured in the United States of America
Designed and edited by Gwen McKee

CONTENTS

PREFACE.. 6

HALE AND HEARTY COCKTAIL BUFFETS......... 7
   Let's Celebrate after the Game 8
   We're Hosting an Open House.....................11
   We're Having an Announcement Party 15
   Come to Our Tree Trimming Party 18
   We Want You to Meet Our Weekend Guests 21

LIGHT AND LOVELY COCKTAIL PARTIES........25
   Come Help Us Celebrate Our Anniversary...........26
   We're Planning a Party under the Stars 30
   Come to Our House after the Theatre..............33
   Join Us for a Cup of Christmas Cheer 35

WHAT A LOVELY WAY TO START THE DAY 37
   Let's Get Together for Brunch 38
   Join Us for a New Year's Day Brunch 41
   Come to My Neighborhood Coffee 45

LOVE IN THE AFTERNOON 49
   You're Invited to an Afternoon Baby Shower........50
   I'm Having a Tea to Introduce Our New Bride 54
   We're Honoring the Graduates with a Tea Dance......57

HEARTWARMING PICNICS 61
   We're Entertaining the Club at a Boat Party 62
   Couples Come! It's a Picnic for Lovers 66
   Let's Tailgate before the Game 68
   It's Snowing! Come for a Fireside Picnic............71

LOVE AT FIRST BITE—FIRST COURSES 73

INDEX 77

PREFACE

Everybody loves hors d'oeuvres, but the shortest chapter in most cookbooks is usually the hors d'oeuvres section. There are dozens of recipe collections featuring specific foods, yet few on hors d'oeuvres. For these reasons, we decided to join forces to write a cookbook starring party pick-up savories and sweets. We have included a chapter on first courses for the occasional formal dinner party, and special hints to make your entertaining easier.

From our hostessing experiences, we learned early that party-giving confidence and peace of mind come from two things: cooking ahead whenever possible rather than preparing last minute tidbits, and planning selections that require little attention once on the table. We added a touch of caviar—a little goes a long way— to several recipes to show what magic it can bring to an otherwise ordinary appetizer. When possible, we designated the number of servings, but sometimes this depends on the hour and the variety of other items.

We collected recipes from many sources. Some were shared by generous friends, others are family heirlooms, and many were created in our own kitchens. After months of searching old files, we found that original recipes are hard to trace. Most change as they spread among cooks until their origins become clouded by time.

Perhaps because we love people, we love parties, and we find parties as endlessly fascinating as people. They afford a marvelous opportunity to exercise your theatrical talents by providing a lovely setting; your culinary abilities by cooking extraordinary food; your creative imagination by planning a festive theme.

The French translation of hors d'oeuvres is "outside the main work"—something extra special. We hope our cookbook will inspire you to make your next party *extra special.*

Jo Barksdale and Mary Leigh Furrh

Hale and Hearty Cocktail Buffets

Let's Celebrate after the Game
We're Hosting an Open House
We're Having an Announcement Party
Come to Our Tree Trimming Party
We Want You to
Meet Our Weekend Guests

Our menus and recipes for cocktail buffets feature foods that are filling enough to serve as a small meal. A large, pretty entree of beef, turkey, or pork with appropriate bread and condiments is the star. A seafood hors d'oeuvre, cheese appetizer, colorful vegetable dish, and other tidbits fill out the menu.

Placing desserts and coffee on a separate table gives an elegant touch of intimacy while helping with the flow of people. If your party is large, use salad-size plates so guests may move away from the table with their refreshments, allowing others to have their turn.

When planning your guest list, invite enough people for a cozy group, but do not include so many that reaching the buffet becomes a problem. Instead, divide your list and have the party on two consecutive nights. One housecleaning and one menu will simplify your preparations and a smaller number will allow you to mingle more with your guests.

Let's Celebrate after the Game

Gretchen's Barbecued Brisket
Food Processor Mayonnaise
Horseradish Mustard
Celebration Chili Dip
Hot Dogs in Cheese Sauce
Guacamole Dip
Pigskin Deviled Eggs
My Grandmother's Sugar Cookies
Chocolate Crunchies

GRETCHEN'S BARBECUED BRISKET
Smoky, tender and filling

1 (5-pound) brisket	*1 (28-ounce) bottle barbecue sauce*
Salt and pepper	*Parsley*

Season brisket with salt and pepper. Cover well with barbecue sauce. Bake 3 hours at 275 degrees uncovered. Turn. Cover tightly with foil. Bake 3 more hours. Remove brisket from sauce. Cool. When cool, slice thin and return to sauce. For party, arrange attractively on platter. Decorate edges with parsley. Serve with hard rolls.

This brisket improves in flavor if refrigerated and allowed to soak in sauce for a few days after cooking. Reheat for party. Serve at room temperature with *Food Processor Mayonnaise* and *Horseradish Mustard*.

FOOD PROCESSOR MAYONNAISE
Fast, foolproof method

1 egg	*¼ teaspoon salt*
1 tablespoon vegetable oil	*1/8 teaspoon Cayenne*
2 teaspoons lemon juice	*1 cup vegetable oil*
1 teaspoon Dijon Mustard	

Place steel blade in food bowl. Blend egg, 1 tablespoon oil, lemon juice, mustard, salt and Cayenne for a few seconds. Continue to run food processor while adding 1 cup oil slowly and steadily through feed tube. Mixture will almost immediately reach consistency of mayonnaise.

HORSERADISH MUSTARD

Stir 1 cup mustard and 4 tablespoons horseradish together. Chill before serving.

CELEBRATION CHILI DIP
Chases the chill on a cold night

1 tablespoon oil
1 pound ground chuck
1 medium onion, chopped
2 tablespoons flour
1 (8-ounce) can tomato sauce

1 cup hot water
5 teaspoons chili powder
1 teaspoon ground cumin
Salt, pepper to taste

Heat oil. Brown meat and saute onion until clear. Sprinkle flour over mixture. Gradually stir in tomato sauce and water. Add seasonings. Simmer 30 minutes, stirring occasionally. Serve hot in chafing dish with corn chips.

HOT DOGS IN CHEESE SAUCE
Tasty and unusual

1 can cream of chicken soup
½ cup milk
½ teaspoon dry mustard
1 teaspoon Worcestershire

1/8 teaspoon Cayenne
½ pound sharp Cheddar cheese
1 pound wieners

Combine soup, milk, mustard, Worcestershire and Cayenne in top of double boiler. Cook over hot water until hot. Add cheese; stir until smooth.
Cut hot dogs into 1-inch pieces and stick a toothpick in each. Pour cheese sauce into a chafing dish and place franks and picks in sauce. You may make cheese sauce ahead and add franks at last minute.

GUACAMOLE DIP
You'll give a cheer for this fast, easy blender dip

2 medium avocados
½ cup sour cream
2 tablespoons chopped onions
2 tablespoons lemon juice

2 tablespoons white wine
1 teaspoon garlic salt
1/8 teaspoon Cayenne
2 teaspoons Worcestershire

Chop avocados into blender. Add remaining ingredients. Puree until creamy. Chill. Serve with raw carrots, cauliflower or other vegetables.

PIGSKIN DEVILED EGGS
They look like little footballs

6 eggs
3 tablespoons mayonnaise
1 tablespoon mustard
1 tablespoon pickle relish

2 teaspoons Worcestershire
1 tablespoon chopped olives
1 teaspoon salt
Pimento strips

Boil eggs 20 minutes. Drain, cool with cold running water; peel. Cut into halves. Remove yolks. Beat yolks with a fork and combine with remaining ingredients except pimento. Put filling in whites. Decorate like footballs by putting one pimento strip lengthways and two crossways on top of egg halves. Makes 12 halves.

MY GRANDMOTHER'S SUGAR COOKIES
Nutmeg and lemon rind give these unusual zip

½ cup shortening
½ teaspoon salt
½ teaspoon grated lemon rind
½ teaspoon nutmeg
1 cup sugar

2 tablespoons milk
2 eggs, beaten
2 cups flour, sifted
1 teaspoon baking powder
½ teaspoon soda

Blend shortening, salt, lemon rind and nutmeg. Add sugar gradually and cream well. Add milk and eggs. Sift flour with baking powder and soda. Add to creamed mixture, blending well. Drop from teaspoon onto greased baking sheet. Let stand a few minutes, then flatten cookies by pressing with a glass covered with a damp cloth. Sprinkle with sugar and bake at 350 degrees 15-20 minutes. Makes 4½ dozen.

CHOCOLATE CRUNCHIES
Your guests can't stop eating them

½ cup oleo or butter
1 cup brown sugar
1 egg, well-beaten
2 (1-ounce) squares unsweetened
  chocolate, melted
1 cup flour, sifted

½ teaspoon baking soda
¼ teaspoon baking powder
½ teaspoon salt
1 cup shredded coconut
1 teaspoon vanilla
1½ cups quick oats, uncooked

Cream butter and sugar. Add beaten egg and melted chocolate. Mix until smooth. Sift together flour, soda, baking powder and salt. Add slowly to mixture. Add coconut and vanilla. Stir in oats. Drop by half-teaspoonsful about 2 inches apart onto a greased baking sheet. Flatten each by criss-crossing with tines of a fork. Bake at 350 degrees 20 minutes. Makes 4½ dozen.

We're Hosting an Open House

Smoked Turkey
Curried Mayonnaise
Linda's Ruby Cheese Mold
Super Shrimp Mold
Spicy Marinated Vegetables
Chafing Dish Pork Balls
Lemony-licious Squares
Mrs. Bowden's Nutaroons
Georgianne's Champagne Punch

SMOKED TURKEY
Serves a crowd

Rub inside of 15-18 pound self-basting, butterball turkey with salt. Sprinkle with black pepper and Lemon Pepper Marinade. Cook in charcoal-water smoker (such as Cajun Cooker) for approximately 8-10 hours. Use meat thermometer to be certain of time. Add hickory chips to fire to increase smoky flavor. Serve with thinly sliced white and whole wheat bread with crusts removed, and *Curried Mayonnaise*.

CURRIED MAYONNAISE

Mix one teaspoon curry powder with one cup mayonnaise. Delicious!

LINDA'S RUBY CHEESE MOLD
A blend of Cheddar and pecans topped with strawberry preserves

1 pound sharp Cheddar cheese,
  grated
2 tablespoons milk
¼ cup mayonnaise (or enough
  to bind mixture)

¼ teaspoon black pepper
Dash of cayenne
2 tablespoons grated onion
1½ cups pecans, finely chopped
Strawberry preserves

Cream cheese, milk and mayonnaise in mixer. Add seasonings and onion. Stir in nuts. Pour into well-oiled pie plate or flat mold; chill. Unmold and spread strawberry preserves over top. Serve with crackers.

SUPER SHRIMP MOLD
A pretty addition to your cocktail buffet

1 (8-ounce) package cream
  cheese, softened
1½ (1-ounce) envelopes unflavored gelatin
½ cup cold water
1 cup mayonnaise
1 tablespoon lemon juice
1 tablespoon grated onion

1 tablespoon chopped parsley
1 teaspoon salt
1 teaspoon Worcestershire Sauce
2 teaspoons Durkee's Famous Sauce
White pepper to taste
Seasoned salt to taste
2 cups shrimp, boiled and diced

Beat cream cheese well. Add gelatin which has been softened in water and
dissolved over low heat in double boiler. Mix in mayonnaise and lemon
juice. Add other ingredients, folding in shrimp last. Pour into well-oiled
1-quart mold. Chill until set. Unmold and serve with crackers. Super!

 A small crochet hook will make an easy job of deveining shrimp.

SPICY MARINATED VEGETABLES
Makes a beautiful, colorful platter

VEGETABLES:
Fresh mushrooms, whole
Carrots, sliced
Zucchini, sliced

Broccoli, broken into buds
Canned artichoke hearts, drained
*whole green beans
asparagus*

VEGETABLE MARINADE:
1 cup olive oil
1 cup red wine vinegar
1 teaspoon garlic powder
1 teaspoon salt

1 teaspoon dry mustard
4 teaspoons sugar
1 teaspoon tarragon
½ teaspoon pepper

Place fresh vegetables and drained artichoke hearts in separate containers.
Combine marinade ingredients, divide into individual containers of vegetables and refrigerate overnight. When ready to serve, drain well and arrange on a platter. Place toothpicks in a separate container. Makes 2 cups.

 *Herb Vinegars: Use 1 cup loosely packed fresh herb leaves per pint of vinegar.
The longer it stands, the stronger the flavor. Strain and bottle in sterilized
glass containers and seal.*

CHAFING DISH PORK BALLS
Serve the leftovers with rice

1/3 cup minced onions
2 tablespoons margarine
1 egg
½ cup milk
½ cup bread crumbs
1¼ teaspoons salt
2 teaspoons sugar
½ teaspoon allspice
¼ teaspoon nutmeg

1 pound ground pork shoulder
2 tablespoons butter or margarine
3 tablespoons flour
1 teaspoon sugar
1¼ teaspoons salt
1/8 teaspoon pepper
1 cup water
1 cup light cream

In large skillet, saute onions in 2 tablespoons margarine until golden. Meanwhile, in large mixing bowl, beat egg; add milk and crumbs. Let stand 5 minutes; add 1¼ teaspoons salt, sugar, allspice, nutmeg, ground pork and sauteed onions. Shape meat mixture into small balls about ½-¾ inches in diameter. Drop some balls into skillet; brown well on all sides; remove to casserole. Repeat until all meat is browned.

Into same undrained skillet, melt remaining margarine; stir in remaining flour, sugar, salt and pepper. Slowly add water and cream. Stir until thickened. Place meatballs in sauce. Serve in chafing dish with toothpicks in small container on side. May be prepared ahead and reheated.

LEMONY-LICIOUS SQUARES
The best lemon square recipe you'll ever find

1 cup butter, softened (no
  substitutions, please)
2 2/3 cups flour
½ cup sugar
4 eggs

1½ cups sugar
4 tablespoons flour
½ teaspoon baking powder
6 tablespoons lemon juice
Confectioners sugar

Mix butter, flour and sugar well. Press into ungreased 9x12-inch pan. Bake at 350 degrees 20 minutes or until slightly brown on edges. Make filling.
  Beat eggs, add 1½ cups sugar gradually, then 4 tablespoons flour and baking powder. Stir in lemon juice. Pour over partly done crust. Cook 20 minutes longer. Sprinkle with confectioners sugar while hot. Cool well before cutting into 1-inch squares. Cool thoroughly on racks. Makes 3 dozen luscious squares.

MRS. BOWDEN'S NUTAROONS
One of my grandmother's best recipes

2 egg whites
1 cup brown sugar

½ teaspoon vanilla
2 cups pecans, chopped fine

Beat egg whites until stiff. Sift brown sugar. Add to eggs, beating in a few tablespoons at a time. Add vanilla and fold in nuts. Drop half-teaspoons onto greased cookie sheet. Bake at 325 degrees 20 minutes. Let dry 20 minutes. Makes 3½ dozen.

 Rose Petals in Ice Cubes: Freeze ice tray half full. Anchor a rose petal with a teaspoon of water; freeze; fill with water and freeze.

GEORGIANNE'S CHAMPAGNE PUNCH
Keep it going by adding more champagne and ginger ale

2 ice ring molds
1 liter ginger ale
1 fifth of champagne

Green grapes
Fresh or frozen peaches

Make ice rings by filling ring molds with water and placing in freezer until frozen. Place in punch bowl. Pour in champagne and ginger ale. Float fruit in punch. Add more of each liquid when needed.

We're Having an Announcement Party

Tenderloin of Beef
Bleu Cheese Butter
Chicken Liver Pâté
Windy's Wonderful Mold
Pat Ross' Chinese Egg Rolls
Sweet and Sour Sauce
Hot Mustard
Hot Asparagus Dip
Chocolate Heaven Cupcakes
Margaret's Spritz Cookies

TENDERLOIN OF BEEF
Elegant presentation, exceptional flavor

½ cup olive oil
1 cup Worcestershire
Lemon pepper

3 (3-pound) beef tenderloins

Make marinade of olive oil and Worcestershire sauce. Sprinkle beef tenderloin with lemon pepper. Marinate approximately 4 hours at room temperature, turning once or twice. Pour off marinade. Start cooking 1½ hours
before serving time at 350 degrees, uncovered. Use meat thermometer and
cook until medium rare (approximately 45 minutes). Let sit about 45 minutes before serving to allow time for juices to set. Slice thin and serve with
toast rounds. Spread with *Bleu Cheese Butter*. Serves 100.

BLEU CHEESE BUTTER

Cream 2 ounces of bleu cheese with 1 stick of real butter (no substitute).
Put into a small decorative mold. Chill. Unmold and serve at room temperature as a spread for beef.

CHICKEN LIVER PÂTÉ
Rich, creamy, melts in your mouth

2 pounds chicken livers
½ cup chopped onion
2 tablespoons butter
½ cup sherry
½ teaspoon salt

½ teaspoon powdered thyme
3 tablespoons anchovy paste
1 (3-ounce) package cream cheese
½ cup soft butter
½ cup chopped parsley

Saute chicken livers and onions in butter until livers are just done. Put
mixture in blender and mix until smooth. Heat sherry until reduced to ¼
cup. Blend into chicken-liver mixture. Beat in salt, thyme, anchovy paste,
cream cheese and soft butter, using mixer. Continue beating until smooth
and well blended. Chill until firm. Shape into a ball. Roll in chopped parsley to coat. Serve with Melba Rounds.

WINDY'S WONDERFUL MOLD
Easy and impressive—your guests will think it took all day to make

1 can beef consomme
1½ tablespoons unflavored
  gelatin
8 ounces cream cheese, softened

Few drops Tabasco
¼ teaspoon garlic salt
1 teaspoon Worcestershire
½ teaspoon seasoned salt

Melt the beef consomme. Take out ½ cup and dissolve gelatin in it. Return to remaining consomme. Pour one half of mixture into a mold and chill until firm. Beat cream cheese in mixer and season to taste with garlic salt, Tabasco, Worcestershire and seasoned salt. Spoon into mold on top of consomme. Chill until firm. Pour rest of consomme on top and chill. Serve with crackers.

PAT ROSS' CHINESE EGG ROLLS
Absolutely the best egg roll recipe

6 tablespoons peanut oil
½ pound pork, finely ground
2 tablespoons soy sauce
2 tablespoons sherry
2 teaspoons salt
Pinch of sugar
2 cloves garlic, minced
½ pound raw shrimp, minced

2 cups celery, chopped
1 cup water chestnuts, chopped
8 scallions, finely chopped
1½ cups bean sprouts
2 tablespoons cornstarch, blended
  with 2 tablespoons water
1 pound egg roll wrappers
Peanut oil for deep frying

Heat 2 tablespoons oil in a large pot and fry pork until it loses its pink color. Add soy sauce, sherry, salt, sugar, garlic, and shrimp. Continue to cook, stirring, until shrimp turns pink and just cooked. Transfer the entire contents to a bowl and set aside. Add 4 remaining tablespoons oil to pan and stir-fry celery 3-4 minutes. Add the water chestnuts, scallions and bean sprouts. Mix thoroughly. Return pork and shrimp mixture to the pan. When juices begin to boil, add cornstarch paste and stir-fry until it thickens. Put filling in bowl and set aside until it is cold. When mixture cools, fill wrappers and deep fry until golden brown. Serve hot, sliced diagonally, with *Sweet and Sour Sauce* and *Hot Mustard*.

SWEET AND SOUR SAUCE

10 tablespoons orange
  marmalade

2 tablespoons cider vinegar
2 teaspoons Worcestershire

Mix together and serve as dip for *Chinese Egg Rolls*.

HOT MUSTARD

Blend 5 tablespoons dry mustard to a paste with 5 tablespoons flat beer and a few drops of vinegar. Serve as dip with *Chinese Egg Rolls*.

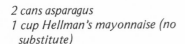

HOT ASPARAGUS DIP
Make it fast in your blender

2 cans asparagus
1 cup Hellman's mayonnaise (no
  substitute)

½ cup Parmesan cheese, finely grated
1 teaspoon lemon juice
1 tablespoon garlic salad dressing mix

Drain asparagus and whip in blender. Add other ingredients, blending after each addition until smooth. Heat in double boiler. Serve in chafing dish with corn chips.

CHOCOLATE HEAVEN CUPCAKES
A chocoholic's dream

FILLING:
6 ounces cream cheese, softened
1/3 cup sugar

1 egg, beaten
4 ounces chocolate chips

Beat cream cheese, sugar, and egg. Stir in chocolate chips. Set aside.

CAKE:
3 cups flour
2 cups sugar
½ cup cocoa
½ teaspoon salt
2 teaspoons soda

2/3 cup cooking oil
2 cups water
2 tablespoons vinegar
2 teaspoons vanilla

Sift dry ingredients. Add oil and other liquids. This makes a thin batter. Spoon into miniature muffin tins lined with "midget" baking cups, pouring them ¾ full. Drop ½ teaspoon filling into center of each. Bake at 350 degrees 20-25 minutes, shifting pans occasionally so cream cheese mixture won't brown. Makes 5 dozen.

MARGARET'S SPRITZ COOKIES
Crisp, buttery, and not too sweet

1 stick butter
¾ stick margarine
¾ cup sugar
1 egg

2½ cups flour
½ teaspoon baking powder
1/8 teaspoon salt
1 teaspoon almond extract

Cream softened butter and margarine with sugar. Add egg. Sift flour once, then re-sift with baking powder and salt. Add to mixture slowly, beating after each addition. Add almond extract. Form into marble-size balls and flatten onto greased baking sheets with hands. Make a criss-cross pattern on each cookie by dipping a fork into flour and pressing it into dough. Bake at 350 degrees 15 minutes or until golden. Makes 4 dozen.

Come to Our Tree Trimming Party

Frosted Ham
Marvelous Mustard
Ann's Bacon-Wrapped Hot Tamales
Seven-Layer Taco Dip
Linda's Sombrero Dip
Camille's Tuna Mold
Pat's Broccoli Dip with Crudités
Chocolate Fondue With Fruit and
Cake Dippers

FROSTED HAM
Frost a canned ham like a cake

3 (8-ounce) packages cream
  cheese, room temperature
½ cup light cream

1 tablespoon prepared horseradish
1 (5-pound) canned ham, baked

Cream the cheese and cream together, adding more cream if necessary for spreading consistency. Add horseradish to taste. (Should be just barely discernable.) Frost top and sides of a baked canned ham and decorate with cherries, olives, or your own special decoration.

MARVELOUS MUSTARD
Great for Christmas gift giving

1 cup cider vinegar
¾ cup dry mustard
1 tablespoon horseradish

3 large eggs
1 cup sugar

Blend vinegar, mustard, and horseradish about 1 minute in a blender. Transfer to a pint jar and let sit overnight. Next day, beat eggs with sugar in top of a double boiler. Add vinegar mixture and cook for about 20 minutes or until it is thick enough to coat the back of a spoon. Makes about 1 quart. Put into 4 half-pint jars for Christmas gifts. The recipe doubles well.

ANN'S BACON-WRAPPED HOT TAMALES
Make a lot when there are men present—easy to do ahead

Cut prepared hot tamales into 3 sections. Wrap each piece with a slice of bacon cut to wrap around it. Broil on each side until bacon is cooked. May be done ahead and reheated.

SEVEN-LAYER TACO DIP
Be sure to try this cold dip—it will bring raves!

1 (16-ounce) can refried beans
1 (10½-ounce) can bean dip
2 tablespoons Jalapeno peppers
10-ounces Monterey Jack cheese,
  grated
10-ounces sharp Cheddar cheese,
  grated
2 cups sour cream
1 package taco seasoning

1 (8-ounce) bottle Picante sauce
2 chopped ripe avocadoes, or
  Guacamole spread
Juice of 1 lemon
1 small onion, finely chopped
2 tomatoes, finely chopped
1 (4.2-ounce) can black olives,
  drained and chopped

In a 2-quart oblong casserole, spread a mixture of refried beans, bean dip and Jalapeno peppers. Sprinkle on Monterey Jack, then Cheddar cheese. Mix sour cream and taco seasoning; smooth on top of cheese. Gently pour Picante sauce over all. This can be made ahead up to this point.

When ready to serve, mix chopped avocadoes with lemon juice. Spoon a layer of avocadoes, onions, tomatoes, and black olives in that order. Serve with an iced tea spoon for dipping with tortilla chips.

LINDA'S SOMBRERO DIP
A new twist to an old favorite

1 pound lean ground beef
1 pound ground sausage

1 pound Velveeta cheese
1 (10-ounce) can Rotel tomatoes

Cook hamburger and sausage till done. Drain and add Rotel; simmer 20 minutes. Stir in cheese until it all melts. Put in chafing dish and serve with Fritos.

CAMILLE'S TUNA MOLD
Also elegant for a gourmet picnic

1 (3-ounce) package lemon Jello
½ cup boiling water
½ cup finely chopped onions
2 (7-ounce) cans white tuna
½ cup Hellman's mayonnaise

1 cup Half-and-Half cream
½ teaspoon salt
¼ teaspoon paprika
¼ teaspoon garlic powder

Dissolve gelatin in boiling water in blender until dissolved. Add chopped onions and blend 30 seconds. Add tuna and mayonnaise; blend slowly. Blend in remaining ingredients. Put mixture into a 4-cup greased mold. Chill 4-5 hours. Unmold and garnish with parsley and lemon bows.

PAT'S BROCCOLI DIP WITH CRUDITÉS
The easiest and the best cold broccoli dip

1 package frozen, chopped
  broccoli
½ cup green onions with tops

½ cup finely minced parsley
Salt and pepper to taste
2 cups Hellman's mayonnaise

Thaw broccoli and squeeze out liquid. Do not cook. Mix all the ingredients together and chill for 24 hours. Serve with raw vegetables.

    Spinach may be substituted for broccoli. If serving with crackers, you may add chopped water chestnuts and mushrooms.

CHOCOLATE FONDUE WITH FRUIT AND CAKE DIPPERS
A fun and delicious dessert

6 (1-ounce) squares semi-sweet
  chocolate
1 cup plus 1 teaspoon cream
1½ cups sugar

½ cup butter
1/8 teaspoon salt
2 teaspoons vanilla

Combine all ingredients except vanilla. Cook over low heat, add vanilla and serve in a fondue pot. Use fondue forks to dip fresh fruit and cake pieces. Fresh fruit should be well drained and brushed with lemon juice to prevent browning. Strawberries, pineapple chunks, mandarin orange segments, cherries, sliced apples, pears, peaches, bananas, kiwi fruit, nut halves, marshmallows, pieces of cake (angel food, sponge, or pound), and Lady Fingers are all delicious dippers.

 Sherried Dates: Soak a (16-ounce) package of pitted dates in 1 cup of cream sherry for 1 day in the refrigerator. Remove and stuff each with a pecan half. Store in airtight container up to a month.

We Want You to Meet Our Weekend Guests

New Orleans Shrimp Rémoulade
Cold Pork Tenderloins with Fruit Garni
Chafing Dish Artichoke Spread
Grace's Spinach Sandwiches
Tempting Tomato Canapés
Strawberries with Chef's Cream Mold and
Grand Marnier Aspic
Mary Alice Bookhart's Creole Lace Cookies

NEW ORLEANS SHRIMP RÉMOULADE
Offer this seafood treat with the sauce in an elegant shell

SHRIMP:
Allow ½ pound per person for an entree; ¼ pound for first course. Cook the shrimp your favorite way and serve with the following sauce.

NEW ORLEANS RÉMOULADE SAUCE:

1 pint Hellman's mayonnaise
1 medium onion, grated
4 tablespoons finely chopped
  parsley
4 tablespoons finely chopped
  Kosher dill pickles

1 finely chopped hard-cooked egg
Juice of 1 lemon
3 tablespoons dry mustard
Garlic salt to taste
Pepper to taste

Grate onion on a paper towel and let it stand until moisture is absorbed. Add it to mayonnaise with remaining ingredients. If it is too thick, add a little juice from the dill pickles. Serve cold with seafood.

 Carrot Curls and Zigzags: Cut thin lengthwise strips from a carrot with a vegetable peeler. To make curls, roll strips up and secure with wooden picks. For zigzags, thread strips onto wooden picks accordion-style. Crisp both by placing them in ice water; remove picks before serving.

COLD PORK TENDERLOIN WITH FRUIT GARNI
A stunning party surprise

3-3½ pounds pork tenderloin

MARINADE:
1 cup sherry
1 cup fresh orange juice
½ cup fresh lemon juice
½ cup olive oil
2 teaspoons grated lemon peel

2 teaspoons crumbled, dried
  marjoram
1 teaspoon cumin seed
1 teaspoon ground ginger
2 bay leaves

Combine ingredients in a large dish or plastic bag. Add pork and marinate 3-4 hours or overnight, turning pork frequently.

TENDERLOIN SAUCE:
Salt and fresh ground pepper
2 tablespoons butter
1 teaspoon Dijon mustard

2 tablespoons red currant jelly
1 (11-ounce) can mandarin oranges,
  drained

Preheat oven to 325 degrees. Pat pork dry with paper towel (reserve marinade). Sprinkle with salt and pepper. Melt butter in Dutch oven over medium heat. Add pork and brown on all sides. Add reserved marinade. Cover and bake, basting often, until thermometer inserted in thickest part registers 165-170 degrees, about an hour. Remove pork from liquid and cool to room temperature. Wrap tightly in foil; refrigerate up to 2 days.

Strain cooking liquid and transfer to small saucepan and refrigerate. Just before serving, discard fat from surface of liquid. Bring cooking liquid to a simmer over medium heat. Stir in mustard and currant jelly. Add mandarin oranges. Remove from heat. Chill.

Slice chilled pork thinly and arrange on tray or platter. Spoon warm sauce over, garnishing with mandarin oranges and parsley. Serves 12.

CHAFING DISH ARTICHOKE SPREAD
Guests think this dish is crabmeat

2 (14-ounce) cans drained
  artichoke hearts
2 cups Hellman's mayonnaise

1 package Good Seasons dry Italian
  dressing mix
½ teaspoon lemon juice

Chop artichoke hearts coarsely and mix with other ingredients; refrigerate until ready to serve—this may be done several days ahead. Serve hot with Melba Toast or Wheat Thins or bagels cut for dipping. Also good cold with crudites.

GRACE'S SPINACH SANDWICHES
A real trend setter—equally good as a dip

1 (10-ounce) package frozen
chopped spinach
½ (8-ounce) can water chestnuts,
finely chopped
¼ cup sour cream
½ teaspoon lemon pepper

½ teaspoon Tony's Creole Seasoning
(or seasoned salt and Cayenne)
3 green onions with stems, chopped
2 tablespoons mayonnaise
1 loaf thin sliced bread (28 slices)

Thaw and squeeze water from spinach. Place it between paper towels and pat dry. Do *not* cook. Mix with other ingredients. Add more sour cream for a spreadable consistency, if needed. Amount of onion and spice may also be increased to taste.

Trim crust from bread and spread spinach mixture on half the slices. Top with other half of slices. Cut sandwiches diagonally, making 4 tiny triangles. Makes 112 sandwiches.

Onion Brushes: Slice off roots and most of tops of several green onions. Then make thin slashes from near center to each end, producing a fringe. Place in ice water to curl ends.

TEMPTING TOMATO CANAPÉS
These look so pretty served with spinach sandwiches

28 rounds of thin white bread
Butter at room temperature
28 thin slices unpeeled ripe tomato

½ cup homemade or Hellman's
mayonnaise
Fresh basil

Bread rounds may be frozen in a plastic bag until morning of the party. Spread a thin layer of butter on bread rounds. Top each buttered round with a tomato slice; garnish with mayonnaise spiced with basil to taste.

Use pimento cheese in place of butter when tomatoes are out of season and not as tasty.

Pickle Fans: Make 3 or 4 lengthwise slices from 1 end of pickle almost to other (don't cut all the way through). Spread slices apart to resemble a fan; press uncut end.

STRAWBERRIES WITH CHEF'S CREAM MOLD
AND GRAND MARNIER ASPIC
Make ahead and enjoy!

1 tablespoon unflavored gelatin
1 tablespoon cold water
2 cups whipping cream,
  unwhipped
½ cup sugar
2 cups sour cream

1 teaspoon vanilla
Strawberries, washed with stems on
1 recipe Grand Marnier Aspic
  (page 31), for garnish
¼ cup almonds, blanched and sliced
  thinly

Soften gelatin in cold water. Combine with cream and sugar in a saucepan and cook over low heat, stirring, until gelatin and sugar are dissolved; do not let it boil. Chill mixture until thickened to consistency of raw egg white. Stir in sour cream and vanilla; pour mixture into a lightly oiled 1½-quart ring mold and chill until firm.

Make aspic. Stir in almonds when consistency of raw egg white. Refrigerate until firm.

To serve, unmold *Chef's Cream* onto a large tray. Spoon firm aspic around base of chef's mold and fill center with strawberries. Arrange some of the strawberries around base with aspic. Garnish with fresh mint leaves. Guests spread some of the mold onto the strawberries and lace cookies with a butter knife.

 Creme Fraîche: Combine 1 cup heavy cream with 1 tablespoon buttermilk. Cover and let stand at room temperature 8 hours or until thick. Keep chilled 6-8 weeks.

MARY ALICE BOOKHART'S CREOLE LACE COOKIES
A much-loved food columnist learned to make these from a creole friend

1 cup Quick Quaker Oats
3 tablespoons flour, unsifted
½ teaspoon baking powder
1 teaspoon salt

1 cup sugar
1 stick butter (no substitutions)
1 teaspoon vanilla
1 egg, beaten

Mix dry ingredients; cut in butter; add vanilla and egg. Mix and refrigerate overnight. Drop marble-size pieces of dough on cookie sheet lined with foil, about 3 inches apart, as they spread during cooking. Bake at 325 degrees about 11 minutes. Do not let them get too dark. Cool just enough to peel cookies off foil, then cool thoroughly and store in an air-tight container. Makes 2-3 dozen cookies.

Light and Lovely Cocktail Parties

Come Help Us Celebrate Our Anniversary

Come to Our House after the Theatre

We're Planning a Party under the Stars

Join Us for a Cup of Christmas Cheer

The food at cocktail parties is lighter than at cocktail buffets. Usually, these affairs take place earlier in the evening when guests are invited to stop by for a bite on their way to dinner or another function. Sometimes a cocktail party is held after an event such as a concert or play. They are an ideal way to celebrate an anniversary or introduce an honored guest.

The emphasis at cocktail parties is on pretty food that stimulates conversation as well as appetites. Some of the hors d'oeuvres may be passed hot from the oven. Be sure to include spreads and dips, however, to avoid too many last-minute preparations.

Most of the recipes in this section are equally good with cocktails in your living room or on your deck before a dinner party. Remember not to serve more than two hors d'oeures before a meal. Otherwise, your guests will lose their appetites.

Come Help Us Celebrate Our Anniversary

Marinated Shrimp Biloxi
Hot Cheddar-Bacon Dip with Sliced Apples
Artichoke and Lemon Tree
Failure-proof Hollandaise Sauce
Vivian Williams' Dressing Balls
Carolyn's Ham Balls
Caviar-Lover's Mold
Marvelous Meringues
Raspberry Filling
Viennese Chocolate Filling

MARINATED SHRIMP BILOXI
Improves with age, so make it early

4½ pounds shrimp
1 small jar capers
Celery seed to taste
4-5 lemons, sliced thin
3 large onions, sliced thin

1 tablespoon horseradish
2 (16-ounce) bottles Italian dressing,
*   pour oil off one bottle*
½ cup red wine vinegar

Cook and clean shrimp. Cool. In a shallow glass dish, put 1 layer shrimp, capers, and celery seed. Completely cover with lemon slices and onion slices which have been separated into rings. Repeat until all are used. End with lemon slices on top. Mix horseradish, Italian dressing, and vinegar. Pour this marinade over shrimp and chill at least 24 hours. Remove from marinade and serve with toothpicks.

HOT CHEDDAR-BACON DIP WITH SLICED APPLES
Easy to make ahead and re-heat

6 slices bacon
8 ounces cream cheese
2 cups grated Cheddar cheese
6 tablespoons cream
1 teaspoon Worcestershire

¼ teaspoon dry mustard
¼ teaspoon onion salt
3 dashes Tabasco
Wedges of red and green apples,
*   unpeeled*

Cook bacon, drain, and crumble. Melt cream cheese in double boiler. Stir in grated cheese and cream. Add remaining ingredients. Add crumbled bacon to melted cheese mixture. Serve in chafing dish to keep warm. Serve with alternating slices of Granny Smith green and Red Delicious red apples—good color appeal and good taste!

ARTICHOKE AND LEMON TREE
A beautiful conversation piece

12 artichokes
2 tablespoons lemon juice

Red leaf lettuce
12 lemons

Clip artichoke points with scissors. Remove prickly portion. Trim bottom stem to make even. Boil artichokes in large pan of water, with lemon juice to prevent discoloring, for 20 minutes. Drain well and cool.

Cut off top of 10-inch styrofoam cone to make it flat on top. Cover cone with lettuce leaves and secure with hairpins. Working from bottom to top, insert wooden picks leaving about 2 inches of pick to hold cooked artichokes. Place artichokes on picks, working from bottom to top of cone. End with 1 artichoke on top. Fill space between with lemons, securing them with wooden picks. Place completed "tree" on large tray with a bowl of *Hollandaise Sauce* on each side for dipping, and an empty bowl in which leaves can be discarded. Serves approximately 150. This may be made 1 day ahead, wrapped with damp dish towel and refrigerated.

FAILURE-PROOF HOLLANDAISE SAUCE
Serve at room temperature

4 egg yolks
1 stick butter

2 tablespoons lemon juice
Salt and pepper

Put egg yolks in a double boiler over hot water (don't let water boil). Divide butter into 3 parts and add to eggs one part at a time. Stir continually until butter melts and thickens. Remove from heat and beat 2 minutes. Add lemon juice, salt and pepper to taste. If it should curdle, add 2 tablespoons boiling water and beat.

This sauce should be served at room temperature. It may be made the day before, but don't reheat it. Take out of refrigerator the morning of the party and it will be room temperature by evening.

 To keep Hollandaise Sauce *at serving temperature, prepare 3 hours before party and pour into a thermos bottle. It will remain lukewarm.*

VIVIAN WILLIAMS' DRESSING BALLS
Eat one and you can't stop

2 (8-inch) pans corn bread
4 slices toast, crumbled
1 cup celery, finely chopped
1 cup onions, finely chopped

½ cup margarine
2 eggs, slightly beaten
1 tablespoon parsley
1 can chicken broth

Make a double recipe of cornbread mix and crumble finely into a large bowl. Add finely crumbled toast. Saute celery and onions in margarine and add to bread mixture. Add eggs, parsley and chicken broth and mix well. Roll into small, firm balls. Place on greased cookie sheet. Bake at 300 degrees 20 minutes or until brown. Shake cookie sheet once in order to brown evenly. May be frozen and reheated. These little balls look attractive in a small bowl or basket lined with a white linen napkin. Makes about 135.

CAROLYN'S HAM BALLS
Delicious sweet 'n sour ham and pork combination

1 pound ground ham
1½ pounds ground pork
2 cups bread crumbs
2 eggs, well beaten
1 cup milk

1½ cups brown sugar
½ cup vinegar
½ cup water
1 teaspoon dry mustard

Mix ham, pork, bread crumbs, eggs and milk and shape into balls. Place in 2-quart casserole in 1 layer. Meanwhile make sauce by mixing brown sugar, vinegar, water and mustard. Pour over balls. Bake 2 hours at 300 degrees, turning once. Makes approximately 40 large or 100 small balls.

CAVIAR-LOVER'S MOLD
For the true aficionado

3 (8-ounce) packages cream
  cheese, softened
¼ cup milk, approximately (to
  thin cream cheese)

1 (2-ounce) jar red caviar
1 (2-ounce) jar black caviar
½ cup green onions, chopped
½ cup hard-boiled eggs, chopped

Beat cream cheese in mixer. Thin slightly with milk until smooth. Pack into 3-cup mold. Chill until firm. Unmold on tray. Place separate bowls of red caviar, black caviar, chopped onions and chopped eggs around tray to use as topping. Place a small spoon beside each bowl. Serve with crackers.

MARVELOUS MERINGUES
Raspberry and Viennese Chocolate Fillings are a perfect combination

4 egg whites
½ teaspoon vinegar
1 teaspoon vanilla

¼ teaspoon salt
1 cup sugar, sifted

Beat egg whites. When frothy, add vinegar, vanilla and salt, beating well after each addition. When egg whites stand in soft peaks, begin adding sugar one tablespoon at a time. Continue beating until stiff but not dry.

Preheat oven to 225 degrees. Cover 2 cookie sheets with brown paper or foil. Drop mixture by tablespoons onto paper. Scoop out centers with teaspoon and build up sides of each meringue so it will hold filling well. Bake 45-60 minutes. Cool well on racks. Makes 2 dozen meringues.

 In making meringues for pies, sweeten to taste by adding separately, Karo syrup and confectioners sugar. This makes a much higher, tastier meringue.

RASPBERRY FILLING

1 cup raspberry preserves
1 tablespoon cornstarch

Sour cream

Melt preserves in small saucepan. Remove small amount to mix with cornstarch in a separate bowl. Add cornstarch mixture to preserves. Cook on low heat until thick. Cool. Use a teaspoon to fill meringues with filling. Top each tart with ½ teaspoon sour cream. Fills 24 meringue shells.

 When whipping cream, use confectioners sugar in place of granulated. The cream is fluffier and holds up longer.

VIENNESE CHOCOLATE FILLING

12 ounces semi-sweet chocolate
  chips
¼ cup boiling water

1 tablespoon instant coffee
1 cup whipping cream, whipped
1 teaspoon vanilla

Melt chocolate in double boiler over simmering, not boiling, water. Stir in coffee which has been dissolved in boiling water. Remove from heat; beat well. Fold whipped cream into chocolate; add vanilla. Fills 24 shells.

 Drop leftover whipped cream by spoonsful onto waxed paper and freeze. When frozen, seal in airtight container.

We're Planning a Party under the Stars

Cathy's Chafing Dish Hamburgers
Dot Ward's Mystery Pizza
Baked Potato Peels with Caviar Dip
Sparkling Fruit Canapés
Charlotte's Grasshopper Cheesecakes

CATHY'S CHAFING DISH HAMBURGERS
Make plenty of these miniatures—they go fast

1 pound ground chuck
2 tablespoons grated onion
1 teaspoon prepared mustard
1 egg
½ teaspoon red pepper

½ teaspoon garlic salt
1 teaspoon salt
1 tablespoon Worcestershire sauce
½ cup flour
Barbecue sauce (your favorite)

Combine all ingredients except last 2. Form into tiny balls ½-inch in diameter. Flatten slightly to resemble hamburgers. Roll lightly in flour; fry in hot fat. Place in chafing dish; mix with warmed barbecue sauce. Serve with miniature buns. Makes 25-30.

 For a quick antipasto, coat a can of good white tuna, unmolded, with mayonnaise and garnish with ripe olives, capers and artichoke hearts.

DOT WARD'S MYSTERY PIZZA
You may never go back to the real thing

2 tablespoons minced onion
1 cup mayonnaise
1 (4.2-ounce) can ripe olives, chopped

2 cups grated sharp Cheddar cheese
2 loaves party rye bread rounds (or rye bread cut into rounds)
Bacon bits

Blend minced onion, mayonnaise, ripe olives, and grated cheese. Spread on bread rounds; sprinkle with bacon bits. Bake 15 minutes at 350 degrees. Makes about 40 little pizzas.

BAKED POTATO PEELS WITH CAVIAR DIP
A tasty, unusual surprise

POTATO PEELS:

2 tablespoons unsalted butter,
  melted
½ teaspoon seasoning salt
¼ teaspoon pepper

Peelings from 6 scrubbed baking potatoes, ¼-inch thick (leave some
  potato on peel), ¾-inch wide,
  2 inches long

In a bowl combine melted butter, seasoning salt and pepper. Brush peels with mixture. Arrange skin side down in one layer on a buttered baking sheet. Bake in preheated 425-degree oven 15-20 minutes, until lightly browned. Turn them and bake 10-15 minutes more or till golden brown.

CAVIAR DIP:

1 pint sour cream
1 (6-ounce) jar red caviar

1 tablespoon minced onion

Gently mix ingredients together. Chill.

SPARKLING FRUIT CANAPÉS
Brown bread with almond butter, glazed with shimmering fruit in aspic

1 loaf thin sliced, brown wheat bread,
  crusted, cut into decorative shapes

ALMOND BUTTER BASE:

4 ounces almond paste
1 cup butter, softened

1 (8-ounce) package cream cheese,
  softened

Beat almond paste till soft. Beat in butter and cream cheese till fluffy. Spread on bread cut-outs; pipe a little paste around outside edges for border. Cover with waxed paper; set aside.

GRAND MARNIER ASPIC:

1/3 cup cold water
1 tablespoon unflavored gelatin
1/3 cup Grand Marnier
2/3 cup cold water

Suggested fruits and nuts: small
  pieces of unpeeled apples or pears,
  halved grapes, orange sections, walnuts, pecans, or almonds

Soak gelatin in 1/3 cup cold water; simmer to dissolve. Add Grand Marnier and 2/3 cup cold water. Refrigerate until partially set (consistency of un-beaten egg white). Place small pieces of thinly sliced or cut-up fruit, and nuts, if desired, on bread cut-outs. Spoon some partially set aspic over fruit to cover. Chill until aspic is set. May be made day before party. Recipe makes 30-40 canapes and doubles well.

CHARLOTTE'S GRASSHOPPER CHEESECAKES
Wonderful to serve at cocktail parties

1 (8½-ounce) package Nabisco Famous chocolate wafers, crushed
3 (8-ounce) packages cream cheese
1½ cups sugar

4 large or extra large eggs plus 1 egg yolk
6 tablespoons green creme de menthe
2 tablespoons white creme de cocoa

Butter 1½-inch muffin tins. Place 1 teaspoon crumbs in tins; shake around to cover bottom and sides. Shake out excess. Cream softened cheese on medium speed of electric mixer; add sugar, then eggs, one at a time. Beat in liqueurs. Spoon mixture into prepared pans; bake at 350 degrees 25-30 minutes. Cool. Add topping.

CHOCOLATE TOPPING:
4 (1-ounce) squares semisweet chocolate, melted and cooled

½ cup sour cream, room temperature

Blend chocolate and sour cream. Place in cake decorator tube and make a swirl on top of each cheesecake. Refrigerate till serving time. Bake several days in advance. Makes 4 dozen.

 When a recipe calls for melted chocolate, place a square in its own wrapper, seam side up, in your microwave for 2 minutes on HIGH.

Come to Our House after the Theatre

Lobster Tail Medallions with Caviar Sauce
Artichoke Heart Flowers
Opening Night Tartare Canapés
Fruit in Persian Melon
Encore Chocolate Truffles

LOBSTER TAIL MEDALLIONS WITH CAVIAR SAUCE
A glorious way to serve lobster

½ lobster tail per person, cooked according to package directions

CAVIAR SAUCE:
1 cup Hellman's mayonnaise *1 teaspoon chopped chives*
1 (2-ounce) jar red or black caviar *1 teaspoon chopped fresh parsley*
1½ tablespoons lemon juice

Stir gently together. To serve, remove lobster tail whole from shell after it has been cooked and chilled. Cut into small rounds and arrange on a bed of greens. Drizzle sauce over lobster tails or serve sauce separately in a bowl in the center of the medallions. Exquisite.

ARTICHOKE HEART FLOWERS
They resemble little flowers with their egg centers

1 (14-ounce) can artichoke hearts *Salt and pepper to taste*
2 eggs, hard-boiled *1 scant teaspoon sugar*
3 tablespoons mayonnaise *¼ teaspoon dill weed*
1 teaspoon prepared mustard *Black olives*

Drain artichoke hearts and cut in half lengthwise. Chop eggs fine. Add mayonnaise, mustard, salt, pepper, sugar and dill weed. Top artichoke hearts with egg mixture. Put a sliver of black olive on end to resemble flower. Makes about 16.

OPENING NIGHT TARTARE CANAPÉS
Serve in fresh mushrooms and cherry tomatoes on a bed of parsley

2½-pound sirloin tip roast, fat
  removed
Juice of 1 large lime
6 tablespoons dry red wine
2 large cloves garlic, minced
¾ teaspoon Tabasco sauce
2 teaspoons dry mustard
1 teaspoon salt
3 tablespoons Worcestershire
1 teaspoon hickory smoked salt

1 teaspoon curry powder
1 teaspoon Heinz 57 Sauce
1 bottle capers (approximately ½-
  ¾ cup)
2 pints cherry tomatoes, tops cut
  off, seeds removed with small
  melonball scoop
2 pints large mushrooms, stems
  removed
Parsley for garnish

Have raw, lean roast put through meat grinder twice and wrapped in white paper. In a large bowl, add remaining ingredients except tomatoes, mushrooms and parsley. Blend mixture thoroughly. Put into prepared tomatoes and mushrooms. Put a small sprig of parsley on top of each and place on a bed of parsley. This can be done several hours ahead of party time if you cover tightly with Saran Wrap and refrigerate. Leftovers can be put into oven or microwaved for lunch the next day. Stuffed mushrooms may be frozen. Makes about 40 tomatoes and 40 mushrooms.

FRUIT IN PERSIAN MELON
A beautiful mixture of fruit

1 large Persian melon
1 fresh pineapple or 1 can of
  pineapple chunks

1 quart strawberries
4 ounces light rum, or to taste
Romanoff Sauce

Cut melon in half and scoop out meat with melon ball scoop. Reserve the shells. Combine melon balls with strawberries and pineapple chunks. Pour rum over fruit, sprinkle with powdered sugar and put back into shells; cover and chill. Serve with *Romanoff Sauce* (page 47).

ENCORE CHOCOLATE TRUFFLES
A microwave chocolate-coffee truffle that can be frozen

12 ounces semisweet chocolate
  chips
4 egg yolks
½ cup coffee liqueur

2/3 cup butter, softened
Cocoa powder, ground almonds,
  chocolate shot or powdered sugar

Melt chocolate in a 1-quart measure on HIGH for 2 minutes. (Chocolate may not look melted.) Stir through with a wooden spoon. Let cool to room temperature. Beat in egg yolks one at a time. Blend in liqueur. Cook on HIGH 30 seconds. Add softened butter to chocolate mixture 1 tablespoon at a time, beating well after each addition. Continue until mixture is light and fluffy—about 4-5 minutes. Cover with plastic wrap and chill 5 hours or overnight. Roll mixture into ¾-inch balls. Garnish with your choice of garnishes. Makes about 5 dozen. Refrigerate until serving time.

Join Us for a Cup of Christmas Cheer

Chafing Dish Lobster
Aunt Katie's Corned Beef Pastries
Beckwith's Sensational Spinach Mold
Skewered Pineapple and Cherries
Crème de Menthe Balls

CHAFING DISH LOBSTER
Lobster tails in a gorgeous wine cheese sauce

*2 packages lobster tails, cooked
  according to package directions*
2 tablespoons butter
2 drops Tabasco

*2 cups (about 8 ounces) shredded
  sharp processed American cheese*
1/3 cup dry white wine

Cook lobster tails and reserve. Melt butter in a double boiler on low heat. Gradually stir in cheese until cheese is melted. (Cheese-butter mixture may appear separated at this point.). Add Tabasco; slowly add wine, stirring constantly until mixture is smooth. Add chunks of lobster tails and stir until heated. Serve in a chafing dish with Melba Rounds or toast cups.

AUNT KATIE'S CORNED BEEF PASTRIES
Spicy corned beef in an easy sour cream roll pastry

1 recipe Sour Cream Pastry
  (page 60)
1 (12-ounce) can corned beef

¼ cup mayonnaise
¼ cup Durkee's Famous Sauce

Chop corned beef up in a bowl. Mix mayonnaise and Durkee's together and add to corned beef, mixing well. Refrigerate until ready to make pastries. (Leftovers make wonderful sandwiches.)

Make crust. Roll to 1/8-inch thickness on a floured board and cut into 2-inch circles. Place a scant teaspoon on each circle; fold over and seal edges with a fork that has been dipped in milk. Place on a greased baking sheet and bake 15-20 minutes in 350-degree oven. Edges will be brown, but pastries have color and taste of homemade rolls. Makes about 5 dozen.

BECKWITH'S SENSATIONAL SPINACH MOLD
Especially pretty at Christmas served with cherry tomatoes,
broccoli, and cauliflower flowerettes

1 teaspoon plain gelatin
½ cup cold water
1 (3-ounce) package lemon Jello
1 cup hot water
1½ teaspoons vinegar
½ cup mayonnaise
¼ teaspoon salt

Dash of pepper
1 (10-ounce) package frozen
   chopped spinach, thawed and
   drained (do not cook)
¾ cup cottage cheese
1/3 cup celery, diced
2 green onions, chopped

Soak plain gelatin in ¼ cup of cold water. Dissolve lemon gelatin and
plain gelatin in the hot water. Add rest of cold water (¼ cup) and beat
in vinegar, mayonnaise, salt and pepper. Refrigerate.

When it begins to congeal, beat with an electric mixer 2 minutes or until a little fluffy. Add spinach, cottage cheese, celery, and onion. Mix well.
Pour mixture into 1-quart mold. Refrigerate until firm.

Unmold and garnish with cocktail tomatoes, broccoli and cauliflower
flowerettes. To serve, spread a little of the mold onto vegetables with a
butter knife. Crackers may also be served.

SKEWERED PINEAPPLE AND CHERRIES
Colorful and delicious

2 fresh ripe pineapples
Sugar for sprinkling

1 (10-ounce) bottle Maraschino
   cherries

Cut 2 fresh, ripe pineapples in half lengthwise, leaving leaves on. Scoop out
meat, leaving ½-inch shell, and being careful not to puncture it. Discard
the tough meat, and cut rest into bite-size pieces. Sprinkle with sugar. Put
a piece of pineapple on a toothpick with a cherry half. Pile back into the
shells, cover and refrigerate until serving time. Arrange the 4 halves on a
large platter to serve.

CRÈME DE MENTHE BALLS
There will be many requests for this recipe

2 cups vanilla wafer crumbs
1 cup pecans, finely chopped
1 cup confectioners sugar

2 tablespoons light corn syrup
½ cup white or green creme de
   menthe

Chop pecans finely in food processor. Set aside in bowl. Place vanilla wafers in the work bowl and chop finely. Add pecans to vanilla wafer crumbs
and mix in confectioners sugar. Add corn syrup to creme de menthe and
blend in with crumb-nut-sugar mixture. Add more creme de menthe or
wafer crumbs for a good consistency if necessary. Chill and form into
small balls; roll in confectioners sugar. Makes approximately 30 balls.

What a Lovely Way to Start the Day

Let's Get Together for Brunch

Join Us for a New Year's Day Brunch

Come to My Neighborhood Coffee

Mid-morning is an especially festive time for a party. The hostess and guests are at their cheeriest before confronting the cares of the day. This is the occasion to decorate informally with colorful table linens and casual arrangements of flowers and fruit. If the weather is sunny, open your curtains; if cold and rainy, build a fire. Guests will be cheered by the orange glow of burning embers as well as your warm hospitality.

Guests at morning parties are hungry, so prepare plenty of filling food. The time span for a coffee or brunch is 10:00 a.m. until 1:00 p.m. These hours mean that for many, a brunch or coffee is the first meal of the day. For others, especially working people attending a morning party on their lunch hour, the gathering serves as lunch. As with all entertaining, the secret is to be prepared.

Let's Get Together for Brunch

Connie's Brunch Bites
Fruits of the Sea Mousse
Miniature Sesame Almond Drumsticks
Frisco's Spinach Dip
Crème de Menthe Grapes
Chocolate Forbiddens
Cinnamon Nut Fillo Pastry

CONNIE'S BRUNCH BITES
Ham and cheese have never looked so pretty together

2 cups Bisquick
¾ cup ham, fat trimmed and
  finely chopped
1 cup sharp Cheddar cheese, grated
½ cup finely chopped onion
½ cup Parmesan cheese, grated

¼ cup sour cream
2 tablespoons snipped fresh parsley
½ teaspoon salt
2 cloves garlic, crushed
2/3 cup milk
1 egg

Mix all ingredients; spread in greased 13x9x2-inch pan. Bake until golden brown in 350-degree oven 25-30 minutes. Cut into 60 one-inch squares.

FRUITS OF THE SEA MOUSSE
Economical because you can use canned shrimp and crab

1 envelope unflavored gelatin
½ cup cold water
1 (10-ounce) can mushroom soup
2 (3-ounce) packages cream cheese
¼ cup onion, minced
¼ cup celery, minced

1 (4.2-ounce) can shrimp, drained
1 (6-ounce) can crabmeat, drained,
  picked and flaked
½ cup fresh mushrooms, chopped
1 cup mayonnaise
1 teaspoon lemon juice

Soak gelatin in ½ cup cold water. Heat mushroom soup and cream cheese together, stirring until smooth. Remove from heat and add soaked gelatin. When cool, add onion, celery, prepared shrimp, crab and mushrooms. Add mayonnaise and lemon juice; stir until well blended. Pour into a greased mold and refrigerate until serving time.

MINIATURE SESAME ALMOND DRUMSTICKS
Luscious little buttery chicken wing drummettes

¾ cup crushed saltine crackers
¼ cup toasted sesame seeds
2 (¼-ounce) packages slivered
almonds (2/3 cup)
1 tablespoon fresh or freeze-
dried chives
½ teaspoon parsley flakes

½ teaspoon thyme leaves
1 crushed bay leaf
1 teaspoon dry mustard
½ teaspoon salt
2/3 cup sweet cream butter, melted
30 chicken wing drummettes

Combine all ingredients except butter and chicken. Dip chicken in melted butter, coat with crumb mixture. Place chicken on greased baking sheet. Bake in preheated 350-degree oven 35-40 minutes or until golden brown.

FRISCO'S SPINACH DIP
Serve leftovers the next day as a spinach casserole

½ stick oleo
1 medium onion, chopped
3 (10-ounce) packages frozen,
chopped spinach, cooked, drained
2 (10½-ounce) cans cream of
mushroom soup

½ teaspoon celery salt
3 drops Tabasco
1½ rolls garlic cheese, sliced
1 cup chopped mushrooms
1 (2¼-ounce) package slivered
almonds

Melt oleo, add chopped onion, cook until clear. Add spinach and stir in mushroom soup and seasonings. Pour half of mixture into greased 2-quart casserole. Top with layer of cheese, then mushrooms, then almonds. Repeat layers. Bake at 350 degrees 40 minutes. Stir well. May be covered and refrigerated when cool. Reheat for party. Serve with Melba Rounds.

CRÈME DE MENTHE GRAPES
Once you've tried these, you'll think of all kinds of ways to use them

1 pound seedless green grapes
½ fifth creme de menthe

1 (1-pound) box confectioners sugar

Soak grapes in creme de menthe 2-3 hours, turning often. Remove from marinade and drain on paper towels. Spread half confectioners sugar on paper towel and roll drained grapes in it. When dry, repeat procedure with sugar. Refrigerate until serving time. May be frozen. Serve on platter with *Chocolate Forbiddens* and *Cinnamon Nut Fillo Pastry*. Makes about 50.

CHOCOLATE FORBIDDENS
Delicious little chocolate morsels with fudge-like centers

CHOCOLATE CRUST:

1¾ cups flour
1/3 cup unsweetened cocoa
  powder
¼ cup sugar

Pinch of salt
¾ cup butter, chilled and cut into
  small pieces
1/3 cup strong coffee, chilled

Sift flour, cocoa, sugar and salt into a large bowl; add butter and blend until consistency of coarse meal. Gradually mix in coffee, adding more if necessary to get a workable dough. Knead a few times. Form into a log, wrap in plastic or foil, and refrigerate several hours or overnight.

Lightly grease tiny 1½-inch muffin pans. Cut dough into 4 pieces. Working with ¼ of dough at a time (keep remainder refrigerated), form into small balls; press against bottom and sides of tart pans.

FORBIDDEN FILLING:

12 ounces semisweet chocolate
  chips, melted
2/3 cup sugar
2 tablespoons butter, melted
2 tablespoons milk

2 teaspoons coffee liqueur
2 eggs, room temperature
½ cup pecans or walnuts, finely
  chopped

Preheat oven to 350 degrees. Combine chocolate, sugar, butter, milk and coffee liqueur in a bowl and blend well. Add eggs; beat until smooth. Stir in chopped nuts. Fill tart shell ¾ full. Bake until filling is set, 12-15 minutes—they will still be a little soft. Let cool in pans. May be prepared ahead and frozen. Makes 4 dozen.

CINNAMON NUT FILLO PASTRY
You can make them ahead and freeze

FILLING:

¾ cup brown sugar
1 teaspoon cinnamon
¼ cup butter, melted

2 cups pecans, chopped
1 egg, slightly beaten

Mix all together well and set aside.

PASTRY:

Frozen fillo pastry

Unsalted butter, clarified

Cut Fillo pastry into 8x3-inch strips. Prepare 1 strip at a time, keeping others covered with plastic wrap. Brush strip with melted butter, using pastry brush. Fold it in half to make a 1½x8-inch strip. Brush with melted butter. Put a small amount of filling in one corner. Fold over to form a triangle. Keep folding for full length of strip. Chill well. Bake in preheated 350-degree oven 15 minutes.

Join Us for a New Year's Day Brunch

Bloody Mary Soup
Lake Charles Caviar Pie
Pâté de Foie Gras Tenderloin of Beef
Artichokes with Sauce Vinaigrette
Black-eyed Pea Quiches
Wheel of Brie with Glazed Almonds
Grand Marnier Cheese Cakes

BLOODY MARY SOUP
A spectacular first course

2 (10¾-ounce) cans Campbell's
   tomato soup
1 (10¾-ounce) soup can water
½ cup fresh lemon juice

½ cup gin
1 tablespoon Worcestershire sauce
1 teaspoon prepared horseradish
½ teaspoon Tabasco

Mix well and heat. Makes about 20 servings in demitasse cups.

Be imaginative in serving dips. Hollowed-out red cabbages, lemon shells, eggplants, red and green peppers, grapefruits or pineapple shells make lovely bowls.

LAKE CHARLES CAVIAR PIE
The addition of crab makes this the most wonderful of caviar pies

8 large eggs, boiled and finely
   chopped
1 cup crabmeat, finely chopped
¼ cup finely chopped green
   onions, tips included

4 tablespoons butter, no substitutes
2 cups sour cream
Salt and pepper to taste
2 (2-ounce) jars caviar, red and/or
   black

Mix eggs, crabmeat and onions together. Melt butter (do not let it brown); cool. Cream with 1 cup sour cream; mix with egg mixture. Add salt and pepper. Place in buttered pie plate. Chill overnight.

    Invert "pie" onto tray; ice with the other cup of sour cream. Decorate with caviar. Serve with toasted bread slices. May be made a day in advance. Serves 35-50 people with this menu.

PÂTÉ DE FOIE GRAS TENDERLOIN OF BEEF
Serve with homemade rolls and Bearnaise Sauce

3-4 pound filet of beef
1 cup dry red wine
3 tablespoons Worcestershire sauce
Juice of 1 lemon
Fresh ground pepper

1 (8-ounce) can Pate De Foie Gras or
  1 cup Mock Pate De Foie Gras
4 tablespoons butter
Homemade pocket rolls
Knorr Bearnaise Sauce or your own

Marinate filet of beef in mixture of wine, Worcestershire, lemon juice and pepper at room temperature 3-4 hours. Remove from marinade. Make a deep slash down length of filet (for pocket), stuff with Pate De Foie Gras. Close pocket with pins and strings. Place in roasting pan; bake at 375 degrees about 45 minutes—use a meat thermometer for desired degree of doneness. Brush often with butter. When cooked, remove from oven; let it rest a half hour before cutting.

To serve, slice meat thinly. Put remaining *Mock Pate De Foie Gras* in a 1-cup mold and serve to "butter" the rolls. Add a thin slice of meat and a little Bearnaise Sauce to "buttered" roll. Bon appetit!

MOCK PÂTÉ DE FOIE GRAS:

½ pound liverwurst sausage
1 (3-ounce) package cream cheese,
  softened
4 tablespoons mayonnaise
1/3 cup cream
1 tablespoon butter, melted

1 tablespoon Worcestershire sauce
1 tablespoon dry sherry
¼ teaspoon salt and pepper
¼ teaspoon curry powder
Pinch of Cayenne pepper
Pinch of nutmeg

Blend all ingredients. Let chill in refrigerator overnight. May also be served with unsalted crackers. Makes 2 cups.

ARTICHOKES WITH SAUCE VINAIGRETTE
Fresh, whole artichokes marinated days in advance—so elegant and easy

3 fresh artichokes
Juice of 1 lemon
½ cup red wine vinegar

1 (16-ounce) bottle Wishbone Italian
  dressing
3-4 lemons sliced for garnish

Trim off tough outer leaves; cook artichokes in boiling, salted water with lemon juice added, until tender. Drain; add vinegar to Italian dressing. Pour over artichokes; refrigerate. May be done 2-3 days in advance. Turn once or twice. To serve, remove from marinade, drain. Serve standing together in middle of tray. Garnish with lemon slices. Serves 30-40.

BLACK-EYED PEA QUICHES
An original from Jo's kitchen—"a special way of securing my luck"

CREAM CHEESE PASTRY:
½ cup butter or margarine   1 cup flour
3 ounces cream cheese, softened

Blend butter and cheese till smooth. Add flour; roll into a ball; chill 1 hour. Shape into 24 small balls; press into greased 1-inch muffin tins.

FILLING:
1 (15-ounce) can black-eyed peas   Dash of seasoned salt
2 medium onions, finely   ½ cup Swiss cheese, grated
  chopped   2 eggs, lightly beaten
2-3 Jalapeno peppers   ½ cup milk
1 beef bouillon cube   1/8 teaspoon nutmeg

Cook peas with 1 onion, pepper, bouillon cube and seasoned salt just enough to season peas. Drain; discard onion and pepper.

To assemble, place a teaspoon of drained peas, ½ teaspoon onion, then ½ teaspoon cheese in each tart shell. Combine eggs, milk and nutmeg and spoon a little into each shell. Bake 8 minutes in preheated 450-degree oven; reduce to 350 degrees and bake 12 minutes more. Serve hot. Bake and freeze, if you wish. Reheat in a 450-degree oven directly from freezer about 10 minutes. Makes 24.

 Slice cherry tomatoes twice vertically, almost to bottom. Fill with cottage cheese or your favorite vegetable dip—a nice compliment to a vegetable tray.

WHEEL OF BRIE WITH GLAZED ALMONDS
Beautiful garnished with red grapes—serve as part of fruit centerpiece

1 (32-ounce) wheel of Brie, room   2 tablespoons powdered sugar
  temperature (reserve container,   ½ cup sliced unblanched almonds
  line with foil)   Red grapes for garnish

Scrape rind from top of cheese. Sift 1 tablespoon powdered sugar evenly over top surface. Arrange sliced almonds over top, pressing firmly into place. Brie can be prepared 1 day in advance up to this point. Return to container; refrigerate. Remove from container; bring to room temperature.

Preheat broiler. Rack should be 6 inches from flame. Place Brie on baking sheet lined with foil. Sift remaining powdered sugar over almonds. Place under broiler, turning as necessary, until top is evenly browned, 1-2 minutes. Watch carefully—sugar caramelizes quickly. Transfer cheese to serving platter, cutting away foil. Arrange small bunches of red grapes around sides of base. Serve with apple and pear slices or buttered brioches.

GRAND MARNIER CHEESE CAKES
Golden morsels with flavored whipped cream, topped with a strawberry

3 (8-ounce) packages cream cheese, room temperature
1 cup sugar
4 large or extra large eggs plus 1 egg yolk
½ cup Grand Marnier

Vanilla wafer crumbs
½ cup whipping cream, whipped
½ cup powdered sugar, sifted
3 tablespoons Grand Marnier
Whole strawberries or Maraschino cherries

Blend first 4 ingredients with mixer till smooth. Place small paper muffin cups in 1½-inch tins. Crumble vanilla wafers in paper cups to cover bottom. Pour mixture in baking cups, filling ½ full. Bake in preheated 350-degree oven 15 minutes. Use straw test for doneness.

Several hours before party, whip cream, add sugar, slowly beat in Grand Marnier. Top each cheese cake with whipped cream and one whole strawberry (washed, dried, and lightly sugared) or cherry. Makes 4 dozen.

 Easy Chocolate Fondue: Heat a 1-pound can Hershey's Chocolate Fudge Topping in a fondue pot.

Come to My Neighborhood Coffee

Shelley's Spiced Tea
Mary's Bacon Sandwiches
Binny Webb's Kolbase Sausage Rolls
Jan Head's Corned Beef Sandwiches
My Grandmother's Cheesies
Strawberries Romanoff
Cinnamon-Chocolate Squares
Butterscotch Dream Bars
Apricot Dainties

SHELLEY'S SPICED TEA
Makes your house smell spicy

1 cup brown sugar
2 sticks cinnamon
1 teaspoon whole cloves
1 lemon, sliced

2 oranges, sliced
4 cups strong tea
½ gallon pineapple juice
1½ quarts cranapple juice

If you have a 40-cup coffee pot, place brown sugar, cinnamon, cloves, lemon, and oranges in coffee grounds container. Put liquids in bottom and perk. If you have no large coffee-maker, put all liquids in a large pot. Make a cheesecloth bag. Fill it with brown sugar, cinnamon, cloves, lemon and oranges and drop it in the liquid. Bring to a boil; simmer 10-15 minutes.

 Besides adding delicious flavor, whole cinnamon sticks make attractive stirrers for hot spiced beverages.

MARY'S BACON SANDWICHES
Crunchy, tart taste

1 (8-ounce) package cream
 cheese, softened
2 tablespoons milk
7 strips bacon, cooked and
 crumbled

3 tablespoons green pepper, chopped
1 tablespoon onion, minced
1 teaspoon Worcestershire
Salt to taste
White bread (about 24 slices)

Beat cream cheese and milk until smooth. Stir in other ingredients. Make sandwiches on white bread. Trim crusts and slice in thirds. Makes approximately 36 finger sandwiches.

BINNY WEBB'S KOLBASE SAUSAGE ROLLS
May be made up to a week ahead and frozen

2 (1-pound) packages Kolbase
  sausage
Dijon mustard

1 egg mixed with 1 teaspoon water
1 recipe Mixer Cream Cheese Pastry

Simmer sausage 10 minutes in water. Cool and peel. Roll ¼ of pastry into rectangular shape slightly longer and wider than ½ of 1 package of sausage. Spread pastry liberally with mustard. Place ½ of 1 package of sausage on this and fold pastry around it. Put on cookie sheet, seam side down. Repeat with remaining 3 sausage halves and pastry thirds. Paint with egg glaze. Cut slashes on diagonal to let out steam; bake at 375 degrees about 20 minutes, or till pastry is lightly browned. Slice into 1½-inch pieces to serve. Makes 40 slices.

MIXER CREAM CHEESE PASTRY:

8 ounces cream cheese, room
  temperature
½ cup butter, room temperature

1½ cups flour
¼ teaspoon salt

Combine all ingredients in mixer. Chill at least 4 hours before using.

 Tomato roses: Make a base by cutting a shallow circle from bottom of tomato; don't sever it completely. Continue cutting a continuous narrow spiral around sides of tomato. Use a gentle sawing motion and taper strip at end to remove it from tomato. Curl strip of peel onto base in the shape of a rose.

JAN HEAD'S CORNED BEEF SANDWICHES
Also good broiled in the oven

1 can corned beef, cut in chunks
6 ounces sharp Cheddar cheese,
  grated
3 teaspoons mustard

2½ tablespoons mayonnaise (may
  need more to soften)
Dash Tabasco

Mix all ingredients in food processor. Make sandwiches with rye bread and mustard. Delicious served from a crock on crackers. If serving in crock, decorate top of corned beef with bay leaves and paprika.

 Radish Accordions: Select long, narrow radishes. Trim off roots and leaves. Make 8-10 crosswise cuts along 1 side of each radish (don't cut all the way through). Place in ice water and chill.

MY GRANDMOTHER'S CHEESIES
A family heirloom

½ cup margarine, softened
½ pound sharp Cheddar cheese,
  grated

2 cups flour
Salt and Cayenne pepper to taste
Sugar

Cream margarine and cheese. Gradually add flour, salt and Cayenne to taste. Roll in a long roll, wrap in waxed paper, and refrigerate overnight. The next day, slice in thin slices and bake on a greased cookie sheet at 350 degrees until light brown, about 15 minutes. When done, sprinkle lightly with sugar and additional Cayenne pepper, if desired. Makes 4½ dozen.

Celery Curls: Trim leaves and cut several long gashes into each rib. Soak in ice water until curled.

STRAWBERRIES ROMANOFF
Adds color to your buffet table

1 quart fresh strawberries
½ cup sugar

1/3 cup orange juice
1/3 cup Grand Marnier

Wash strawberries; drain on paper towels. Place in a bowl, leaving stems intact. Combine sugar, orange juice and Grand Marnier. Pour over berries and refrigerate for no longer than 3 hours. Meanwhile make sauce.

ROMANOFF SAUCE:
1 cup whipped cream
4 tablespoons powdered sugar

3 tablespoons Grand Marnier
3 tablespoons orange juice

Whip cream and flavor with remaining sauce ingredients. At serving time, carefully drain strawberries. Place sauce in a small bowl in center of a round tray with berries arranged around bowl. Serve with toothpicks in a small container nearby.

CINNAMON-CHOCOLATE SQUARES
Delicious with coffee

2 cups flour
1 teaspoon baking powder
1½ cups sugar
4 teaspoons cinnamon
½ cup margarine, softened
1 whole egg

1 egg yolk
1 egg white, slightly beaten
1 (6-ounce) package semi-sweet
  chocolate pieces
½ cup pecans or walnuts, chopped

Sift together flour, baking powder, 1 cup sugar, 3 teaspoons cinnamon. Add margarine, whole egg, and egg yolk. Blend well on low speed. Turn into greased 11x7x¾'' pan. Spread evenly with back of a spoon. Beat egg white slightly. Brush white over mixture with a pastry brush. Combine remaining ½ cup sugar, 1 teaspoon cinnamon, chocolate pieces, and nuts. Sprinkle over top. Bake in pre-heated 350-degree oven 25 minutes. Cool. Cut into squares. Makes 3 dozen.

BUTTERSCOTCH DREAM BARS
A rich, satisfying sweet

1 (6-ounce) package butterscotch
  morsels
¼ cup margarine
1 cup brown sugar
2 eggs

¾ cup flour
1 teaspoon baking powder
¾ teaspoon salt
½ teaspoon vanilla
½ cup pecans or walnuts, chopped

Melt butterscotch morsels and margarine over hot (not boiling) water. Remove from heat. Stir in brown sugar. Cool for 5 minutes. Place in mixer bowl. Beat in 2 eggs. Sift together and add gradually flour, baking powder, and salt. Stir in vanilla, then nuts. Spread in greased 13x9x2'' pan. Bake at 350 degrees 25-35 minutes. Makes 2 dozen 2-inch squares.

APRICOT DAINTIES
They have a tangy taste that compliments this menu

2 (6-ounce) packages dried apricots
1 (14-ounce package grated
  coconut

1 can sweetened condensed milk
Powdered sugar

Grind apricots. Work in grated coconut with fingers. Stir in condensed milk. Pinch off a small amount at a time and make into small balls. Roll in powdered sugar to coat.

Love in the Afternoon

You're Invited to
an Afternoon Baby Shower

I'm Having a Tea
to Introduce Our New Bride

We're Honoring the Graduates
with a Tea Dance

An afternoon tea is among the most elegant modes of entertaining. This is your chance to use your finest table linens and china. Arrange or buy an exquisite floral centerpiece for your table, because above all, a tea must be beautiful.

For this reason, food served at teatime must be especially pretty. We have gathered recipes that taste as good as they look; they are both delicious and appropriate to make your party memorable. Teatime tidbits, which are much less spicy than cocktail party pick-ups, consist mostly of dainty sandwiches and sweets. Guests eat less at this time of day, so you may prepare accordingly.

Although the formal service of tea is not the elaborate ritual of former days, hostesses still serve it in their loveliest teapots. Nowadays, however, they also offer punch or wine. Friends may be asked to "pour."

You're Invited To
an Afternoon Baby Shower

Snappy Chicken Balls
Asparagus Sandwiches Mimosa
Natchez Mushroom Tea Sandwiches
Honey's Pretty Pineapple Sandwiches
Celery With Leftover Cheese
Emerald Bay Kiwi Tartletts
Lynn's Shortnin Bread Cookies
Old Southern Lemon Mint Cookies
Charlotte Charles' Apricot Tea Squares

SNAPPY CHICKEN BALLS
So pretty piled high in a glass dish, decorated with little yellow flowers

2 cups cooked chicken, chopped
   finely
1½ cups almonds, chopped finely
1 tablespoon finely chopped
   green onion
4 tablespoons Major Grey's
   chutney, chopped

1 (8-ounce) package cream cheese,
   softened
¼ cup mayonnaise
2 teaspoons curry powder
Salt to taste
1 cup coconut

Combine chicken, almonds, green onion and chutney. In a separate bowl, blend cream cheese, mayonnaise and curry powder. Combine chicken mixture and cream cheese mixture. Chill. Shape into bite-size balls. Roll each ball in grated coconut. Refrigerate, covered, until ready to serve. Garnish with tiny yellow and white flowers or candied orange peel. Makes 80-90 balls and will keep 3 days.

ASPARAGUS SANDWICHES MIMOSA
Pretty arranged spoke-pattern around the mushroom sandwiches

28 asparagus spears, fresh or
   canned
3 ounces cream cheese, softened
1 tablespoon mayonnaise

1 cup Parmesan cheese
1 loaf thin sliced bread, crust
   removed
Butter, melted

Steam asparagus spears until just tender; drain well. Roll each slice of bread between waxed paper with rolling pin to flatten. Spread thinly with cream cheese mixed with mayonnaise. Sprinkle 1 teaspoon Parmesan cheese over cream cheese. Place asparagus spear on each end of bread slice and roll up. May be frozen at this point. Wrap tightly in waxed paper; place in container. To serve, place seam side down on baking sheet; brush with melted butter; bake 10-12 minutes at 400 degrees. Makes 28.

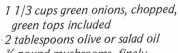

NATCHEZ MUSHROOM TEA SANDWICHES
Dainty, delicious sandwiches that freeze well

1 1/3 cups green onions, chopped, green tops included
2 tablespoons olive or salad oil
¾ pound mushrooms, finely chopped

1 tablespoon flour
½ cup sour cream
1 tablespoon lemon juice
Salt and pepper to taste
2 loaves thin sliced bread

Saute onions in oil until soft; add mushrooms. Cook over low heat 5 minutes; stir in flour; cook 1 minute. Stir in sour cream and lemon juice. Salt and pepper to taste. Cool. Prepare bread by trimming crust; roll flat with rolling pin. Spread mixture on thinly; roll up. Wrap tightly in waxed paper. Refrigerate or freeze. To serve, cut each sandwich into 3 sections. Place seamside down on buttered baking sheet. Bake in preheated 325-degree oven until golden. Makes about 168 sandwiches.

HONEY'S PRETTY PINEAPPLE SANDWICHES
Make these pretty sandwiches ahead and freeze them

2 (8-ounce) packages cream cheese, softened
½ cup crushed pecans or walnuts
1 (8-ounce) can crushed pineapple, drained

Cream (to thin spread)
2 loaves yellow or green tinted bread, thin sliced
1 (10-ounce) jar green Maraschino cherries, drained (optional)

Cream cheese. Add pecans and crushed pineapple; thin for spreading with cream. Prepare bread by removing crust. Place each slice of bread between sheets of waxed paper and flatten with rolling pin. Spread cheese mixture on bread. Cut cherries in half and place down one whole end of bread. Roll; wrap tightly in waxed paper; freeze. At serving time, slice into thin sandwiches. Makes about 280 sandwiches.

 For rolled sandwiches, if bread is not fresh, you will have difficulty rolling it. Try covering it with damp paper towels before placing between waxed paper.

CELERY WITH LEFTOVER CHEESE
Delicious way to prevent cheese spoilage

½ fifth dry red wine
1 gallon crock with cover

1 bunch celery
Leftover cheese

Keep a covered crock containing a half bottle of red wine in your refrigerator. Add any cheese that might be in danger of spoiling. When ready to use, remove some cheese and mash with a little of the red wine. Use to stuff prepared celery and other fresh vegetables such as mushrooms. Sprinkle over salads, spread on crackers. Or try filling celery with *Lazy Day Crock of Cheese* (page 67).

EMERALD BAY KIWI TARTLETTS
Kiwi fruit atop a lime curd filling in a versatile almond pastry crust

Lime Curd Filling
Almond Pastry *tart shells*

½ pint whipping cream, whipped
Sliced kiwi or green grapes

To assemble, spoon *Lime Curd Filling* into tart shells. Add whipped cream on top. Place a small section of sliced kiwi or a green grape on whipped cream. Makes 24 tarts.

ALMOND PASTRY CRUST:
½ cup (1 stick) unsalted butter,
  softened
1/3 cup sugar
1/3 cup ground almonds

2 egg yolks
½ teaspoon vanilla
¼ teaspoon salt
1 1/3 cups flour

Beat butter till fluffy. Beat in sugar, almonds, egg yolks, vanilla and salt until blended. Stir in flour just until blended. Divide dough into 24 balls. Place in 1½-inch greased tart pans. Lightly press to cover bottom and sides. Prick dough with fork; chill ½ hour. Bake in preheated 350-degree oven 15-18 minutes. Cool; carefully remove tart shells. Can be made 1 week in advance and placed in tins. This delicious crust can be used for any filling requiring a prebaked, sweet crust.

LIME CURD FILLING:
1 teaspoon unflavored gelatin
1 tablespoon light rum
1 egg, lightly beaten
2/3 cup sugar

½ stick unsalted butter, softened
1 lime, rind and juice, ground to-
  gether
¼ cup sour cream

Soften gelatin in rum. Set aside. Combine egg, sugar, butter, rind and juice of lime in top of double boiler. Cook, stirring often with wire whisk, until mixture is thick enough to coat back of spoon. Remove from heat; stir in gelatin mixture; add sour cream. Cover surface with waxed paper or plastic wrap; refrigerate overnight.

LYNN'S SHORTNIN BREAD COOKIES
Decorate like tiny little crackers

2 cups flour
1 cup butter (no substitutions)

½ cup confectioners sugar

Mix above ingredients well. Chill dough; roll out to ½-inch thickness between waxed paper. Cut with a 1-inch square cookie cutter. Prick 3 times with a regular fork to resemble tiny crackers. Bake 5 minutes at 325 degrees then turn oven to 300 degrees. Bake 20-30 minutes until golden brown. Put into cookie tins. Makes about 4 dozen cookies.

OLD SOUTHERN LEMON MINT COOKIES
Mint jelly on lemon cookies

2½ cups flour
¼ teaspoon baking soda
1 teaspoon salt
1 cup butter or margarine
½ cup sugar

½ cup light brown sugar
1¼ teaspoons fresh lemon juice
1 egg
1 teaspoon lemon rind, grated
Mint jelly for garnish

Preheat oven to 375 degrees. Sift salt, baking soda and flour. Set aside. Cream butter and both sugars. Mix in lemon juice and egg; add flour mixture and lemon rind, blending well. Form into 1-inch balls; place 1 inch apart on cookie sheet lined with foil. Make an indentation on top of each cookie with tip of a teaspoon. Fill dent with mint jelly. Bake 10-15 minutes. Makes about 6 dozen.

 When cutting marshmallows or chopping dates, dip your scissors in water and cut them wet; they won't stick.

CHARLOTTE CHARLES' APRICOT TEA SQUARES
Cut into larger squares for a colorful, delicious dessert

CRUST:
1 cup flour
½ cup butter (no substitutions)

1/3 cup light brown sugar, packed
½ cup chopped pecans

Combine all except pecans with a mixer. Stir in pecans. Press into ungreased 9x13x2-inch pan. Bake in preheated 350 degree oven till barely browned.

APRICOT FILLING:
2 (8-ounce) packages cream cheese,
  softened
½ cup sugar
2 large eggs
¼ cup milk

¼ cup fresh lemon juice
1 teaspoon grated lemon rind
1 teaspoon vanilla
1 (7¾-ounce) jar apricot junior
  baby food

Cream cheese with sugar; add lightly beaten eggs, milk, lemon juice and lemon rind. Mix well. Pour over partially baked crust. Stir apricots; lightly spoon over cream cheese mixture. Swirl apricots with a fork, being careful not to disturb filling underneath. Bake in preheated 350-degree oven until filling is set, 25-30 minutes, using straw test. Cool; cut into 1-inch squares with a knife dipped in hot water. Refrigerate or freeze. Makes about 60.

I'm Having a Tea
to Introduce Our New Bride

Anycolor Punch
Jo Lynn's New Orleans Benedictine Sandwiches
Janie Brister's Green Bean Sandwiches
Tiny Biscuits With Love Apple Slices
Mary Leigh's Spiced Pecans
Mary's Snowballs
Romantic Raspberry Chocolate Meringues
Jeannine Hudson's Date-Nut Cookies
Dainty Pink and White Heart-shaped Mints

ANYCOLOR PUNCH
The addition of Jello makes it possible to vary the color and flavor

4 cups sugar
12 cups water
1 (3-ounce) package Jello

1 (46-ounce) can pineapple juice
Juice of 12 lemons
1 teaspoon almond extract

Bring sugar and water to a boil and add any flavor (for color) Jello to dissolve. Add pineapple juice, lemon juice and almond extract. Add enough water to make 2 gallons of punch. Serves 35.

JO LYNN'S NEW ORLEANS BENEDICTINE SANDWICHES
Add more mayonnaise and use as a dip or celery stuffer

2 thin slices onion
½ medium cucumber, peeled
  and sliced
8 ounces cream cheese, room
  temperature

2 teaspoons mayonnaise
Dash of garlic salt
Dash of Cayenne
2-3 drops green food coloring
1 loaf thin sliced white bread

Mince onion and cucumber in blender. Combine cream cheese and mayonnaise with mixer. Add onion, cucumber, seasonings, and food coloring; mix on low speed. Refrigerate until thick. Make sandwiches; trim crusts; cut into triangles. Makes about 54.

JANIE BRISTER'S GREEN BEAN SANDWICHES
Raves!

1 can string beans, vertical pack
1 (8-ounce) bottle Italian dressing
½ cup Durkees

½ cup mayonnaise
1 loaf fresh, thin sliced bread,
  crust trimmed

First day: Drain can of string beans; marinate overnight in Italian dressing. Second day: Cut crust from bread; spread with mixture of mayonnaise and Durkees. Drain beans. Place 3 beans on 1 slice of bread; roll up like a jelly-roll and secure with toothpicks. Place in a covered container. Refrigerate overnight. Third day: Cut rolls in 3 sandwiches, removing picks. Will make as many sandwiches as you have beans.

TINY BISCUITS WITH LOVE APPLE SLICES
Divine topped with a dab of Curry Mayonnaise

1 recipe of your favorite biscuits
  cut to cocktail size
1 pint cherry tomatoes

Curry Mayonnaise (page 11)
Parsley

Split biscuits in half. Cut cherry tomatoes (often called love apples) into 3 horizontal slices. Make mayonnaise. To assemble, place a slice of cherry tomato on a biscuit half with a dab of Curry Mayonnaise on top. Garnish with a tiny sprig of parsley.

MARY LEIGH'S SPICED PECANS
So good you may want to double the recipe

2 cups pecan halves
1½ tablespoons butter or
  margarine

1 teaspoon salt
2 teaspoons soy sauce
1/8 teaspoon Tabasco sauce

Melt butter in 13x9x2-inch pan. Add pecans and stir. Toast in 300-degree oven 30 minutes, stirring occasionally. Add salt, soy sauce and Tabasco and toss well with pecans. Serve hot or cold. Makes 2 cups.

MARY'S SNOWBALLS
Pretty and easy

1 white or yellow cake mix or
  a purchased sponge cake
Grated coconut

1 box Betty Crocker Fluffy White
  Frosting mix or a recipe of
  7-minute frosting

Bake a sheet cake by package directions or buy a sponge cake. If baking, cool cake thoroughly. Break cake into walnut-size pieces. Roll in fluffy white frosting, then in coconut.

ROMANTIC RASPBERRY CHOCOLATE MERINGUES
Versatile because of Jello base—try experimenting with other flavors

3 egg whites
1½ ounces raspberry Jello
¾ cup sugar
1/8 teaspoon salt
1 teaspoon white vinegar

1 (6-ounce) package semisweet
  chocolate chips
½ cup pecans or walnuts, finely
  chopped

Beat egg whites until they begin to get stiff. Add gelatin gradually, blending thoroughly. Add sugar a little at the time; beat until stiff peaks form. Beat in salt and vinegar. Fold in chocolate chips and nuts. Drop by half full teaspoon on foil-lined baking sheets. Bake 20 minutes at 250 degrees. Turn off heat and leave in oven 3 hours without opening door. To garnish, you may dip the tops in a little melted chocolate, or before baking, add a little shaved chocolate or a chocolate chip to top of cookie. These will hold their shape. Makes approximately 80.

JEANNINE HUDSON'S DATE-NUT COOKIES
A charming tea cookie

1 stick butter or margarine
1 cup sugar
1 teaspoon vanilla
1 egg, well beaten

1 cup chopped dates
1 cup chopped pecans
2 cups rice crispies
Powdered sugar

Melt butter in skillet. Add sugar, vanilla and dates to well beaten egg. Add mixture to butter in skillet. Cook 5 minutes on low heat stirring constantly. Remove from heat; add pecans and rice crispies. Mix well and roll into balls. Toss the balls in powdered sugar. Makes 3 dozen.

DAINTY PINK AND WHITE HEART-SHAPED MINTS
These can be made ahead and frozen

5½ tablespoons butter, room
  temperature
1 (1-pound) box powdered sugar

2½ tablespoons evaporated milk
12 drops oil of peppermint
Few drops red food coloring

Work butter into sugar with a fork. Mix in milk and oil of peppermint. If dough is too stiff, add a little more milk. If too thin, add a little more sugar. Divide in half and color one half with red food coloring. Put into molds. When hard, pop them out of molds and place between layers of waxed paper. Place in boxes to freeze or refrigerate. Makes about 100 small thin mints.

We're Honoring the Graduates with a Tea Dance

Catawba Punch
Strawberry Sandwiches
Emily's Hawaiian Ham Sandwiches
Graduation Cheese Petit Fours
Jo's Mother's Secret Divinity
Judy's Chocolate Crinkle Cookies
Mrs. Williams' Pecan Pies
Beth's Apricot Baskets

CATAWBA PUNCH
The color of vintage champagne

2 bottles white grape juice   *1 bottle club soda*
1 large bottle 7-Up or ginger ale

All bottles should be as close in size to the grape juice bottle as possible. Have all liquids well chilled. Pour ingredients over ice in a punch bowl. During the party, alternate liquids as punch is being used; pour in 7-Up or ginger ale and follow with club soda. Add a little grape juice each time you add the other liquids; taste as you go. You may add champagne if you wish—a little champagne goes a long way.

STRAWBERRY SANDWICHES
Serve with a basket of frosted strawberries

½ cup confectioners sugar   *1 loaf thin sliced bread*
1 stick softened butter   *Fresh strawberries (2 pints or more)*

Cut washed and dried strawberries into 2 or 3 slices; drain. Cream confectioners sugar and butter together. Cut bread into 2-inch rounds; spread with mixture. Place a thick slice of strawberry on each. Use more sugar if not sweet enough. Garnish serving tray with pretty green leaves. Place basket of frosted strawberries in center or to side. Two rounds from one slice of bread makes approximately 56 sandwiches.

To frost strawberries: Wash, dry strawberries, leaving stems on. Dip strawberries into beaten egg white, then in granulated sugar. Beautiful!

EMILY'S HAWAIIAN HAM SANDWICHES
A delicious mixture that really stretches ham

*1½ cups cooked ham, finely
  chopped
½ cup chopped green onions,
  with some of green tips
1 teaspoon prepared horseradish
½ teaspoon Dijon mustard*

*1 cup whipping cream, whipped
3 tablespoons mayonnaise
Salt and pepper to taste
1 loaf thin sliced bread—brown
  or white*

Combine ham with all ingredients except bread. Spread on bread with crust removed. Cover with another piece of bread; cut each sandwich 3 times into finger sandwiches. Makes about 37.

GRADUATION CHEESE PETIT FOURS
Ice and decorate like little cakes

*2 (5-ounce) jars Old English
  cheese
1 egg, slightly beaten*

*¾ cup oleo
1 teaspoon Durkees (or more to
  taste)*

Soften cheese and oleo. Add beaten egg and Durkees to taste, mixing well. Remove crust from day-old thin sliced bread. Make a 3-deck sandwich by spreading one slice with cheese mixture, add another slice bread; repeat until you have 3 slices of bread. Cut sandwich into 4 squares. Ice top and four sides with cheese mixture. Decorate as you would petit fours with olives and pimentoes. Bake in preheated 375-degree oven 5-8 minutes. Watch carefully. Makes about 36.

JO'S MOTHER'S SECRET DIVINITY
The recipe is out for the first time

5 cups sugar
1 cup white Karo syrup
1 cup hot water
5 egg whites

2 teaspoons vinegar
1 cup chopped nuts
1 teaspoon vanilla

Blend sugar, Karo syrup, and water together in saucepan. Put on medium heat until syrup begins to boil. Do not stir. Cook to hard-boil stage (265 degrees). In another bowl, beat 5 egg whites until stiff peaks form. Pour syrup *slowly* over egg whites while beating with electric mixer. When you have 1 cup syrup left, add vinegar; keep pouring and beat until thick. When candy loses its shine, add vanilla and nuts. Drop by teaspoon onto waxed paper. Makes about 150 pieces.

Do not make this on a rainy day. The secret is in the very slow pouring of syrup and the addition of vinegar to make it fluffy. Heavenly!

JUDY'S CHOCOLATE CRINKLE COOKIES
They look so pretty and taste like brownies

½ cup vegetable oil
4 ounces unsweetened chocolate,
  melted
2 cups granulated sugar
4 eggs

2 teaspoons vanilla
2 cups unsifted flour
2 teaspoons baking powder
½ teaspoon salt
1 cup confectioners sugar

Mix oil, chocolate and granulated sugar. Blend in 1 egg at a time till well mixed. Add vanilla; stir in flour, baking powder and salt; chill overnight.

Preheat oven to 350 degrees. Drop dough by teaspoon into confectioner's sugar—don't attempt to shape yet. Coat lightly with confectioner's sugar—this makes it crinkle. Pick up, roll into a ball, and roll again in confectioner's sugar. Place 2 inches apart on greased baking sheets. Bake 10-12 minutes. Do not overcook. They will be a little soft to the touch. Makes about 4 dozen small cookies.

MRS. WILLIAMS' PECAN PIES
Everybody loves these!

1 recipe Cream Cheese Pastry
  (page 43)
1 egg
¾ cup brown sugar

1 tablespoon butter, melted
1 teaspoon vanilla
2/3 cup coarsely chopped pecans

Beat egg with wooden spoon. Add sugar, melted butter and vanilla; mix well. Stir in pecans. Pour into prepared shells. Bake at 325 degrees 20 minutes. Cool before removing. Makes 24 tarts.

BETH'S APRICOT BASKETS
An ambrosia-like mixture in a sour cream crust

SOUR CREAM CRUST:

1 cup butter, room temperature   ½ teaspoon salt
1 cup sour cream   2 cups flour

Cream butter; add sour cream and salt; mix well. Gradually stir in flour—dough will be slightly soft. Roll into a ball and cover with plastic wrap. Chill 4 hours.

FILLING:

1 cup apricot preserves   10 Maraschino cherries, drained
1 cup flaked coconut   and chopped
½ cup pecans or walnuts, chopped   Confectioners sugar

Combine all ingredients, mix well and set aside. Place ¼ of chilled dough on floured board; roll to 1/8-inch thickness. Keep remaining dough chilled until ready to roll. Cut dough into 2-inch squares; spread each with scant teaspoon of fruit mixture. Starting with a corner, carefully roll each square like a jellyroll; seal ends with milk. This leaves 2 ends open with some of mixture showing. Place on greased baking sheet, seam side up. Bake at 350 degrees 15-20 minutes or until tips are lightly browned. Let cool. Sift confectioners sugar over them. Makes about 5 dozen.

Heartwarming Picnics

We're Entertaining the Club
at a Boat Party
Couples Come! It's a Picnic for Lovers
Let's Tailgate before the Game
It's Snowing! Come for a Fireside Picnic

*W*hat could be more fun than a picnic? Most of the work is done in advance and the hostess has the pleasure of preparing food in her kitchen and serving it at a different location. The setting may be as exciting as a tailgate picnic in the stadium parking lot before the big game, or as relaxing as a boat party on a calm day. You may even celebrate winter's first snowfall with a fireside picnic.

If you plan to travel far from home, you will need to take dishes that will stay cool in an ice chest. Since there will be no possibility of reheating, you must round out your menu with food that may be served at room temperature. With these necessities in mind, we have planned menus and selected recipes to help you enjoy this casual way of entertaining.

We're Entertaining the Club
at a Boat Party

Wheel of Cheddar Cheese
Assorted Crackers
Green Grapes, Sliced Apples, Sliced Pears
Golden Isle Shrimp
Kathy's Exotic Tea Eggs
Green Goddess Dip with Asparagus Dippers
Mix and Match Dessert Breads
Singapore Brandied Cherries

GOLDEN ISLE SHRIMP
Luxurious picnic fare

2 pounds shrimp, shelled, deveined   Lemon slices and parsley

Place shrimp in boiling salted water. Return water to a boil and boil 1 minute, or until just firm. Drain shrimp, toss in the marinade, cover and chill 12-24 hours, stirring occasionally. Transfer drained shrimp to a serving bowl and garnish with parsley and lemon slices. Serves 4.

MARINADE:
¼ cup wine vinegar
2 teaspoons Dijon mustard
2/3 cup olive oil
½ cup finely chopped green
* onions, using green tips also*
½ cup finely chopped green pepper

1 small garlic clove, crushed and
* minced*
1 teaspoon Worcestershire
1 teaspoon fresh lemon juice
Salt and pepper to taste

In a blender, combine vinegar and mustard. Add all the oil in a slow stream until combined. Transfer mixture to a bowl; add remaining ingredients. Combine well and mix with shrimp.

To serve individual portions of caviar attractively, heat back of a metal spoon, press it into an ice cube and fill depression with caviar. Use a plastic spoon to scoop the caviar, as it should never touch a metal or be served on metal.

KATHY'S EXOTIC TEA EGGS
An exciting change from the usual stuffed eggs

6-8 eggs
2 tablespoons dark soy sauce
1 whole star anise
½ teaspoon salt

3 teaspoons of tea (Spice Island's
Formosa, Earl Gray—a smoky tea—,
or any black oriental tea)

Boil eggs 20 minutes over low heat; cool in water. When cool, drain and tap shells all over with back of a teaspoon until the shell is completely cracked. Do not peel.

Place cracked eggs in a saucepan with last 4 ingredients and enough water to cover. Simmer 15 minutes. Cool. Refrigerate overnight still covered in water in which they were cooked.

Drain; wrap individually in plastic until ready to use. To serve, carefully peel eggs. Whites of eggs will be marbled with dark lines. Cut into quarters. These will keep a week in the refrigerator.

 To avoid overcooking the tips of asparagus spears, prop the tips up out of the water with a piece of crumpled foil.

GREEN GODDESS DIP WITH ASPARAGUS DIPPERS
Looks beautiful in a hollowed-out cabbage shell

DIP:
1 clove garlic, minced
½ teaspoon dry mustard
1 teaspoon Worcestershire sauce
2 tablespoons anchovy paste
3 tablespoons tarragon wine vinegar

3 tablespoons minced green onions
1/3 cup minced parsley
1 cup Hellman's mayonnaise
½ cup sour cream
1/8 teaspoon black pepper

Blend all ingredients in a blender. Cover and refrigerate. Will keep for several days. Makes 2 cups.

CABBAGE SHELL:
Cut a slice from bottom of a large cabbage. Hollow out space in top of cabbage to hold a custard cup. Fill with dip.

ASPARAGUS DIPPERS:
Trim asparagus stalks at stem end to equal lengths. Blanch 2-3 minutes, depending on thickness. You want them still crunchy. To blanch, place a few at a time in rapidly boiling water. Don't let them get limp! Plunge immediately into cold water to stop cooking process. Drain and dry with paper towels. Wrap in paper towels, then in plastic, and refrigerate. May be done up to 6 hours in advance.

MIX AND MATCH DESSERT BREADS
Guests will enjoy trying different breads with different butters

VANILLA BREAD:

1 (1-ounce) package dry yeast
¼ cup lukewarm water
1/8 teaspoon sugar
1¼ cups lukewarm water
1/3 cup instant nonfat dry milk

2½ tablespoons vanilla
1 tablespoon sugar
1 teaspoon salt
4 cups flour

Dissolve yeast in ¼ cup lukewarm water with 1/8 teaspoon sugar added for 15 minutes or until foamy. Combine 1¼ cups lukewarm water, dry milk, yeast mixture, vanilla, 1 tablespoon sugar, and salt. Stir in 2 cups flour. Beat on low speed of mixer 1 minute. Beat in other 2 cups flour very slowly, ½ cup at a time, until a soft dough is formed. Knead on a floured board 1 minute. Let stand 10 minutes, knead a few times, adding flour if needed till smooth and elastic, but not sticky. Put dough in buttered bowl, turning to coat with butter. Cover with plastic wrap. Let rise till double in size, approximately 1½ hours.

Punch down gently and shape into a loaf. Place in buttered loaf pan. Cover and let rise to top of pan. Bake in preheated 350-degree oven 50 minutes or until done. Cool in pan on a rack 10 minutes. Turn out on rack and cool 10 minutes more. Delicious with *Vanilla* or *Chocolate Butter*.

CHOCOLATE BREAD:

2 (1-ounce) packages dry yeast
½ cup lukewarm water
1/8 teaspoon sugar
½ teaspoon baking soda
¼ cup water
1 cup lukewarm water
1/3 cup instant nonfat dry milk

1/3 cup plus 1 tablespoon sugar
2 teaspoons vanilla
1½ teaspoons salt
4 cups flour
2 ounces unsweetened chocolate,
  melted and cooled
1 cup chopped pecans or walnuts

Dissolve yeast in ½ cup lukewarm water, with 1/8 teaspoon sugar added for 15 minutes or until foamy. Dissolve baking soda in ¼ cup water. Combine 1 cup lukewarm water, dry milk, yeast mixture, sugar, vanilla, and salt. Stir in 2 cups flour. Add melted chocolate and baking soda mixture. Beat on low speed 1 minute. Beat in 2 cups flour very slowly, ½ cup at a time or until soft dough is formed. Knead on floured board 1 minute. Let stand 10 minutes. Knead a few times, adding flour if needed till smooth and elastic. Knead in nuts. Place dough in buttered bowl and turn to coat with butter. Cover with plastic wrap and let rise till double, approximately 1½ hours.

Follow preceding instructions from "Punch down. . ." in *Vanilla Bread*.

VANILLA BUTTER:

1 stick unsalted butter, room
  temperature
1 cup confectioners sugar, sifted

2 teaspoons vanilla extract
1 ounce cream cheese
Pinch of salt

Cream butter and sugar together. Add vanilla and salt. Cream mixture with cream cheese. Put in a 1-cup butter mold.

CHOCOLATE BUTTER:

1 stick unsalted butter, room
  temperature
1 cup light brown sugar

1 ounce unsweetened chocolate
2 teaspoons vanilla
1/8 teaspoon salt

Cream butter and sifted brown sugar together. Melt chocolate. Cool slightly. Add with vanilla and salt. Put in a 1-cup mold.

 Vanilla Extract: Place 2 split vanilla beans in ½ pint of inexpensive brandy and age for 1 week.

SINGAPORE BRANDIED CHERRIES
You can use canned, but fresh are so elegant in this easy-to-do recipe

1 pound fresh bing cherries,
  pitted

4 ounces red currant jelly
2 ounces brandy

Mix cherries and currant jelly. Refrigerate several hours. When ready to serve, add brandy.

 To make really gourmet coffee, add about 10 grains of salt and 2 or 3 tiny slivers of butter to the grounds in the top of your percolator.

Couples Come! It's a Picnic for Lovers

Alabama Shrimp Chowder
Cupid's Favorite Hamburgers on the Grill
Parmesan Cheese Potato Chips
Petite Deli Dills
Lazy Day Crock of Cheese
B. Stringer's Easy New Orleans Pralines
Basket of Fruit and French Bread

ALABAMA SHRIMP CHOWDER
You will want to make it a part of your permanent files

1 pound fresh mushrooms
1½ cups water
2½ teaspoons salt
¼ cup fresh chopped onion
¼ cup melted butter

¼ cup flour
1/8 teaspoon freshly ground pepper
2½ cups milk
½ cup whipping cream
2 cups chopped cooked shrimp

Combine mushrooms, water and 1 teaspoon salt in saucepan and bring to a boil. Reduce heat and cover. Simmer 10 minutes; drain, reserving liquid. Saute onion in butter in saucepan till tender; stir in flour well; add salt and pepper. Mix well; stir in reserved liquid gradually, blending until smooth; add milk gradually and cook, stirring constantly, until mixture comes to a boil and thickens. Remove from heat; stir in cream, shrimp and mushrooms. Chill thoroughly. Serve in cups garnished with parsley. Serves 6-8.

CUPID'S FAVORITE HAMBURGERS ON THE GRILL
Order tiny bakery buns—enjoy the aroma of meat sizzling on the grill

1 pound ground round steak
1 (3-ounce) jar Smithfield ham,
  or deviled ham
Dash of Worstershire

Salt and fresh ground pepper
Roquefort or Bleu cheese
Dry red wine
Butter

Blend ham spread with ground steak. Add Worcestershire, salt and pepper to taste. Mold hamburger mixture around small pieces of cheese. Cover hamburgers with wine in a dish. Cover and refrigerate about 3 hours.
　　Cook on grill brushing often with marinade mixed with a little melted butter. Serves 5-6. This can be made into small balls for a cocktail party.

PARMESAN CHEESE POTATO CHIPS
Wrap in foil and reheat on the grill

Spread potato chips on baking sheet and sprinkle with Parmesan cheese. Bake in preheated 400-degree oven 5 minutes or until very hot. Wrap in foil; reheat over grill for the picnic.

PETITE DELI DILLS
A miniature version of the famous Deli Dills

1 (32-ounce) jar dill pickles
4 slices bologna or any processed
  cold cuts

3 slices processed American or any
  Cheddar cheese
Mayonnaise

Cut dill pickles in half lengthwise and scoop out center. Coarsely chop bologna and cheese; mix with enough mayonnaise to moisten. Put into each pickle shell. Mask with a little more mayonnaise. Makes about 30.

LAZY DAY CROCK OF CHEESE
After a "start," something wonderful to do with leftover cheese

1 pound sharp Cheddar cheese
3 ounces cream cheese, softened
1½ tablespoons olive oil

1 teaspoon dry mustard
1 teaspoon garlic salt
2 tablespoons brandy

Blend grated Cheddar and cream cheese; add oil, mustard, garlic salt, and brandy, blending well. Pack into a crock, cover, and refrigerate for a week before using. Serve at room temperature. Makes about 3 cups.

To add to crock: Add any firm cheeses, grated, with small amounts of oil, cream cheese, or green olives for consistency. You may also add brandy, port, beer, kirsch, sherry to taste. Let age a few days again. Use every week or two, always leaving part of original mixture to keep crock going.

B. STRINGER'S EASY NEW ORLEANS PRALINES
A soft praline that can be made bite size—easy to work with

1 pound light brown sugar
¾ cup evaporated milk

Few grains of salt
2 cups pecan halves

Mix ingredients together in heavy saucepan. Cook over low heat stirring constantly until sugar dissolves. Continue cooking over medium heat to soft ball stage (236F.) stirring constantly. Cool slightly; beat until mixture begins to thicken. Drop rapidly from spoon onto foil or waxed paper. If mixture gets too hard, add a few drops of milk and stir—you do not have to reheat. Makes about 20 large pralines.

Let's Tailgate before the Game

Touchdown Pork Tenderloin
Deviled Eggs'a la Caviar
Mary B.'s Miniature Boursin Quiches
Winning Vegetable Salad
Dynamite Sticks
Ellen's Cheese Log
Snickerdoodles
Jan's Jewels

TOUCHDOWN PORK TENDERLOIN
Take to picnic in disposable tray—serve at room temperature

¼ cup soy sauce
2 tablespoons brown sugar
2 ounces bourbon
1 (3-pound) pork tenderloin
1 tablespoon dry mustard

1 tablespoon vinegar
½ cup catsup
1 tablespoon soy sauce
½ teaspoon curry powder

Combine soy sauce, brown sugar, and bourbon. Marinate pork in mixture for 1 hour, turning once. Remove meat from sauce. Barbecue over low heat or bake in 325-degree oven 1 hour, basting with marinade every 10 minutes. When cool, cut diagonally into thin slices. Mix dry mustard, vinegar, catsup, soy sauce, and curry. Serve over pork.

DEVILED EGGS À LA CAVIAR
Adds a gourmet touch to your picnic

8 hard-boiled eggs
Mayonnaise
Salt, pepper to taste

1 cup sour cream
1 (2-ounce) jar black caviar, drained
1 (2-ounce) jar red caviar, drained

Cut eggs in half lengthwise. Remove yolks. Mash and moisen with mayonnaise. Season with salt and pepper. Frost eggs with sour cream. Sprinkle with black and red caviar. Makes 16.

MARY B.'S MINIATURE BOURSIN QUICHES
They're marvelous served at room temperature

Cream Cheese Pastry *(page 43)*
¾ cup grated Swiss cheese
¼ cup chopped green onions
¼ cup chopped ripe olives
¼ cup diced fresh tomato

3 eggs
½ cup whipping cream
1 (5-ounce) package Boursin spice cheese

Make pastry and line tiny muffin tins by pinching off a ball of dough and pressing it into each tin, forming to fit with your fingers. Sprinkle ½ cup Swiss cheese on bottom of pastry shells. Mix green onions, olives and tomatoes together and sprinkle over Swiss cheese. Cream eggs and Boursin cheese in mixer. Add cream gradually and spoon over vegetables. Sprinkle with remaining ¼ cup Swiss cheese. Bake in 350-degree oven 25 minutes or until golden. Let stand 5 minutes before removing from pans. Cool on wire racks. Makes 24 miniature quiches.

WINNING VEGETABLE SALAD
Carry in an ice chest

3 (17-ounce) cans English peas, drained
3 stalks celery, chopped
1 (2-ounce) jar pimentos

2 medium onions, sliced
2 (8-ounce) cans water chestnuts, drained and sliced

MARINADE:
1 cup vinegar
1 cup sugar

½ cup corn oil
Salt and pepper to taste

Marinate vegetables overnight in refrigerator. Place in tightly covered plastic bowl. Carry to the picnic in an ice chest.

DYNAMITE STICKS
They keep for weeks in a metal container

1 (20-ounce) loaf extra thin sliced bread

2 sticks margarine
Reese's Lemon Pepper Marinade

Slice each piece of bread into three strips with an electric knife or serrated blade knife. Leave crusts on. Melt margarine. Paint both sides of each strip with melted margarine, using a pastry brush. Place on ungreased cookie sheets. Sprinkle lightly with lemon pepper marinade (Careful—it's hot!) on both sides of each strip. Bake slowly in 200-degree oven 2-3 hours until strips are dry and crisp. Turn strips over with spatula at least once during cooking period. Store in metal containers. These keep for weeks and are nice to have on hand for drop-in guests as well as to take on a picnic.

ELLEN'S CHEESE LOG
Tuck into your ice chest

1 (8-ounce) package cream
  cheese, softened
2 teaspoons horseradish
1 teaspoon Worcestershire
Few drops Tabasco

½ cup chopped pecans
1 jar dried sliced beef cut fine
  with scissors
Parsley flakes

Beat cream cheese in mixer. Add other ingredients. Form into a log. Roll in parsley flakes. Chill. Serve with crackers.

SNICKERDOODLES
A classic cinnamon cookie

1 cup shortening
1½ cups sugar
2 eggs
2¾ cups sifted flour
2 teaspoons cream of tartar

1 teaspoon baking soda
1 teaspoon salt
2 tablespoons sugar
2 teaspoons cinnamon

Cream together shortening, sugar, and eggs. Sift together flour, cream of tartar, soda, and salt. Add to creamed mixture, blending well. Chill dough.
    Roll into walnut-size balls. Roll in mixture of 2 tablespoons sugar and 2 teaspoons cinnamon. Bake on ungreased baking sheet about 10 minutes at 400 degrees. These cookies puff up at first but flatten out with a crinkled top. Makes about 5 dozen.

JAN'S JEWELS
So good and so easy you'll be amazed

4 dozen graham crackers
1 stick butter
1 stick margarine

¼ cup sugar
1 cup pecans, chopped

Grease cookie sheet. Separate graham crackers along dividing lines until there are 4 dozen in all. Arrange on cookie sheet with sides touching. Melt butter and margarine and add sugar. Bring to a boil and continue to boil for exactly 2 minutes. Have chopped nuts ready. Spoon butter mixture carefully over graham crackers. Smooth with knife if necessary. Sprinkle pecans on crackers. Bake at 350 degrees 10 minutes. When brown, lift crackers with spatula and place on foil to cool.

It's Snowing!
Come for a Fireside Picnic

Strawberry Snow Daiquiries
Swiss Cheese Fondue
Thousand Island Dip with Crudités
Appetizer Rubens
Annette's Peanut Butter Fudge Drop Cookies
Anytime Brandied Fruit
Snow Ice Cream

STRAWBERRY SNOW DAIQUIRIES
Higher, fluffier, stays frozen longer than crushed ice

*1/3 cup frozen unsweetened
strawberries, thawed
1/3 cup rum
2 tablespoons lemon juice*

*1 tablespoon superfine granulated
sugar
1 bowl fresh snow (amount
depends upon texture of snow)*

In a blender, combine strawberries and rum; add lemon juice and sugar. Put mixture into a chilled bowl; gradually whisk in snow until mixture is thick. Serve in a chilled glass. Makes 1 drink.

SWISS CHEESE FONDUE
Romantic and fun on a snowy day

*1 pound imported Swiss cheese,
grated
1 tablespoon flour
1 cup dry white wine*

*1 clove garlic
Salt and pepper
Nutmeg
Cubes of crusty French bread*

Dredge grated Swiss cheese thoroughly with flour. Bring dry white wine almost to a boil in a Fondue pot rubbed with a garlic clove on top of the stove. Add cheese gradually, stirring constantly with a fork until all is melted. Add salt, pepper and nutmeg to taste. Serve with cubes of crusty French bread to dunk into cheese with fondue forks.

THOUSAND ISLAND DIP
Serve with crudités—also makes a good salad dressing

Mix 1/3 cup *New Orleans Remoulade Sauce* (page 21) with 1/3 cup tomato catsup. Chill.

APPETIZER RUBENS
Man-pleasing sandwiches

Party rye bread
Horseradish Mustard *(page 9)*
Thinly-sliced corned beef

1 (16-ounce) can sauerkraut, drained
1 (14-ounce) can stale beer
Swiss cheese, sliced

These can be made ahead and broiled at cocktail time. Drain most of juice from sauerkraut. Pour beer over sauerkraut in small saucepan; simmer 20-30 minutes. Drain well. Place bread slices on cookie sheet. Spread each slice with mustard, a slice of corned beef, and a small mound of sauerkraut. Top with a slice of Swiss cheese. Broil 3 inches from heat until cheese melts and is puffy brown.

ANNETTE'S PEANUT BUTTER FUDGE DROPS
Taste as wonderful as they sound

2 cups sugar
1 stick butter or margarine
½ cup milk
3 tablespoons cocoa

½ cup peanut butter
3 cups 1-minute Quaker Oats
1 cup chopped nuts
1 teaspoon vanilla

Mix first 4 ingredients together and bring to a boil. Boil rapidly 1 minute—this is important, so be sure to time it. Remove from heat; add at once the peanut butter, oats, chopped nuts and vanilla. Stir and drop quickly from a teaspoon onto waxed paper. Makes 4 dozen.

ANYTIME BRANDIED FRUIT
Dip from it any time—add to it any time—give it as gifts

1 (2-gallon) stone crock with a lid
1 fifth of brandy

Sugar
Fruits in season

Place brandy in crock. As fruits come into season, put them into crock with equal amount of sugar (1 cup sugar for each cup fruit). Omit any fruits with seeds such as blackberries. For first week, stir with a wooden spoon every day, as the sugar tends to go to the bottom. This does not need to be refrigerated. Keep covered; stir well after each addition.

Suggested fruits: Fresh or canned pineapple (drained), canned mandarin oranges (drained), seeded orange segments, strawberries, seedless grapes, figs, fresh pitted cherries, apricots, peaches, Kiwi fruit.

SNOW ICE CREAM
A superlative concoction—even good without addition of brandied fruit

1½ cups sifted confectioners sugar
1 cup light cream
1 tablespoon vanilla to taste

1 large bowl fresh snow (amount
depends upon texture of snow)

Combine sugar, cream and vanilla. Whisk in snow gradually until ice cream is well mixed and fluffy. If too thin, add more snow. If too thick, add more cream. Add additional sugar and vanilla to taste. Serve plain or with brandied fruit from your crock. Serves about 4.

Love at First Bite
First Courses

In spite of the casual lifestyle most of us lead, there are times when an elegant formal dinner party, featuring several courses, is in order. Even when entertaining informally, some people prefer to serve a first course followed by the entree and dessert.

The customary presentation of a first course is to serve it on a salad-size plate on top of a place plate. You may have this arranged before the guests are seated. The easiest way is to serve your party opener in another room before your guests sit down at the table. Soups listed in other chapters also make delicious first courses.

Servings must be small because of the dinner to follow. If your entree is heavy, make the first course light. The reverse is true when your main course is light.

CAVIAR POTATOES
Unusual first course—something different!

8 small new potatoes	2 tablespoons chopped onion
½ cup sour cream	2 hard-boiled eggs, chopped
½ teaspoon salt	1 (2-ounce) jar black caviar
¼ teaspoon pepper	1 (2-ounce) jar red caviar
Dash of cayenne	Chopped parsley

Boil potatoes until tender, about 20 minutes. Drain well. Cut off small piece of skin and carefully scoop out most of pulp with demi-tasse spoon or melon ball scoop. Whip pulp in mixer with sour cream. Add seasonings, onion and eggs. Fill shells with filling. Spoon caviar on top, using black caviar on half and red on other half. Sprinkle with parsley. Serve 1 black and 1 red potato on each plate at room temperature. Garnish with sprigs of parsley. Serves 4.

STUFFED GRAPE LEAVES WITH AVGOLEMONO SAUCE
May be prepared up to 3 days ahead and refrigerated

2 onions, finely chopped	¼ cup parsley, finely chopped
¼ cup finely chopped celery	Salt and pepper to taste
2 tablespoons butter	1 (1-pound) jar of grape leaves
½ pound round steak, ground	1 cup beef broth
½ pound lamb, ground	Juice of 1 lemon
¼ cup uncooked rice	½ cup dry white wine
1 tablespoon mint, finely chopped	Avgolemono Sauce

Cook onion and celery in 1 tablespoon butter until clear. Place meat in a bowl. Add onion and celery. Add rice, mint, parsley, salt, and pepper. Blend well. Rinse grape leaves carefully under cold running water in a colander, separating leaves gently. Dry gently and place one at a time on flat surface, shiny side down. Place small amount of filling in center of each leaf and roll tightly from stem end toward point of leaf. Arrange rolled leaves in layers in heavy saucepan. Add broth, lemon juice, and remaining butter. Pour in wine and cover with a heavy plate directly on leaves to prevent them from opening. Cook one hour over low heat. Transfer 3 or 4 leaves to each salad-size plate. top with *Avgolemono Sauce* and serve as a first course. Serves 12.

AVGOLEMONO SAUCE:

4 egg yolks	1 cup cooking liquid from stuffed
Juice of 1 lemon	grape leaves

Beat egg yolks well. Add lemon juice and gradually stir in hot liquid. (If there is not a cup of liquid remaining in pan after leaves are removed, add more broth and bring to a boil.) If made ahead, reheat very slowly over hot water to keep sauce from curdling, or serve at room temperature.

SHIMMERING EGGS IN ASPIC
A dazzling show stopper

1 teaspoon salt
1 teaspoon vinegar
4 small or medium eggs
1½ tablespoons unflavored gelatin
1/3 cup water
1 1/3 cups chicken broth

2 tablespoons sherry
1 tablespoon lemon juice
¼ teaspoon fresh dill
Salt and pepper to taste
2 or 3 black olives
4 bread rounds, toasted

Fill heavy frying pan about 2/3 full of water. Add salt and vinegar. Let come to a boil, then reduce heat. Break eggs, one at a time, into saucer. Slip each carefully into simmering water. When ready, whites should be firm, yolks creamy soft. Remove from water with a buttered skimmer and trim edges. Cool.

Soften gelatin in water. Heat chicken broth and add softened gelatin, sherry, lemon juice and dill. Salt and pepper to taste. Place 2 tablespoons gelatin in each individual ramekin that has been well greased. Cut thin round slices of skin from black olives to resemble truffles. Place 1 or 2 pieces with the skin side down in the aspic. Chill until firm. Let remaining aspic cool at room temperature. When refrigerator aspic is firm, place eggs carefully in aspic face down. Cover with additional aspic and chill. Also chill remainder of aspic in flat pan.

To serve, carefully remove eggs from molds, place on toasted bread rounds on chilled plates. Garnish with remaining firm aspic cut in tiny cubes. If desired, place a slice of ham, or *Chicken Liver Pate* (page 15) on bread rounds before topping with egg mixture. Makes 4 servings.

 Drawn Butter: Add 1 tablespoon flour to 5 tablespoons melted butter. Dissolve a chicken bouillon cube in 1 cup boiling water and stir into flour mixture. Bring to a boil and add salt to taste. Delicious for fish and shellfish.

SEAFOOD ON ICE
An impressive assortment of seafood on the half shell

6 half oyster shells per person
Oysters
Clams
Fresh, chilled crabmeat
Cold, boiled shrimp

Cold lobster
Smoked salmon
Lemon wedges and parsley
New Orleans Remoulade Sauce,
(page 21)

For each person, fill a large soup plate with crushed ice. Bury a small glass container in center for sauce. Space 6 oyster half shells equally a-round container. Fill each shell with a different seafood (an oyster in one, a clam in another, and small amounts of crab, shrimp, lobster, and smoked salmon in the others.) Place *New Orleans Remoulade Sauce* in the center container. Garnish with lemon wedges and parsley.

SHRIMP DIJON
Guaranteed to win you raves

1½ pounds raw shrimp, peeled and deveined

MARINADE:
1 cup olive oil
½ cup white wine
½ cup chopped onion
2 cloves garlic, minced

¼ teaspoon pepper
1 tablespoon lemon juice
3 shallots, chopped

DIJON SAUCE:
2 tablespoons margarine
2 tablespoons flour
½ cup milk
½ cup chicken broth
2 tablespoons Dijon mustard

¼ teaspoon pepper
½ teaspoon salt
1 tablespoon lemon juice
2 tablespoons margarine, melted
Chives, chopped

Place shrimp in flat dish. Combine all marinade ingredients and pour over shrimp; refrigerate several hours, turning frequently. Remove shrimp from marinade with slotted spoon and drain on paper towels.

Make sauce by melting margarine and gradually stirring in flour to make a smooth paste. Add milk and chicken broth gradually, stirring constantly. Slowly add Dijon mustard, pepper, salt and lemon juice; cook till smooth and thick. Melt remaining 2 tablespoons margarine in flat dish in broiler. Add shrimp and broil 4 inches from source of heat 3-4 minutes on each side until pink and tender. Place shrimp on individual serving plates and spoon mustard sauce on top. Sprinkle with chives. Serves 4.

CRABMEAT À LA VERNER
Equally good as an entrée or stuffing for flounder

1 pound fresh or canned crabmeat
1 stick butter, melted
1 (10½-ounce) can cream of
  mushroom soup
¼ cup sherry

1 raw egg
2 hard-boiled eggs, grated
1 teaspoon Tabasco sauce
½ cup toasted bread crumbs
Parmesan cheese, grated

Mix all ingredients except bread crumbs and cheese. Pour into 4 well-greased ramekins. Top with bread crumbs and cheese. Bake at 350 degrees approximately 25 minutes.

ARTICHOKE HEARTS ROQUEFORT
Bleu cheese spiked with wine creates a rich taste

1 (10-ounce) can artichoke hearts
8 ounces cream cheese, softened
2 ounces bleu cheese, softened

¼ cup white wine
½ teaspoon lemon juice
Freshly grated Parmesan cheese

Drain artichoke hearts and rinse well under cold, running water. Beat cheeses together until well blended. Add wine and lemon juice; mix well. Stir in artichoke hearts. Grease 4 ramekins and fill ¾ full with mixture. Sprinkle with Parmesan cheese. Bake in 350-degree oven approximately 40 minutes. Cool 5 minutes before serving. Serves 4. Can be made in the morning and reheated for your dinner party.

INDEX

BEVERAGES AND SOUPS

Chowder, Alabama Shrimp 66
Coffee, Gourmet 65
Daiquiries, Snow 71
Punch, Anycolor 54
Punch, Catawba 57
Punch, Georgianne's Champagne 14
Soup, Bloody Mary 41
Tea, Shelley's Spiced 45

CAKES AND DESSERTS

Bread, Chocolate 64
Bread, Vanilla 64
Cheesecakes, Charlotte's Grasshopper 32
Cheese Cakes, Grand Marnier 44
Chocolate Forbiddens 40
Cupcakes, Chocolate Heaven 17
Fondue, Chocolate 20
Ice Cream, Snow 72
Mary's Snowballs 55
Pastry, Cinnamon Nut Fillo 40

CANDIES AND COOKIES

Apricot Dainties 48
Apricot Tea Squares, Charlotte Charles' 53
Butterscotch Dream Bars 48
Chocolate Crinkle Cookies, Judy's 59
Chocolate Crunchies 10
Cinnamon-Chocolate Squares 48
Creme de Menthe Balls 36
Creole Lace Cookies, Mary Alice Book-
   hart's 24
Date Nut Cookies, Jeannine Hudson's 56
Dinivity, Jo's Mother's Secret 59
Jan's Jewels 70
Lemon Mint Cookies, Old Southern 53
Lemony-licious Squares 14
Meringues, Marvelous 29
Meringues, Romantic Raspberry
   Chocolate 56
Mints, Dainty Heart-Shaped 56
Nutaroons, Mrs. Bowden's 14

Peanut Butter Fudge Drops,
   Annette's 72
Pralines, B. Stringer's Easy New
   Orleans 67
Shortnin Bread Cookies, Lynn's 52
Snickerdoodles 70
Spritz Cookies, Margaret's 17
Sugar Cookies, My Grandmother's 10

CHEESE

Brie, Wheel of with Glazed Almonds 43
Butter, Bleu Cheese 15
Celery with Leftover Cheese 51
Cheese Log, Ellen's 70
Cheesies, My Grandmother's 47
Crock of Cheese, Lazy Day 67
Dip, Hot Cheddar-Bacon 26
Fondue, Swiss Cheese 71
Mold, Linda's Ruby Cheese 11
Mold, Windy's Wonderful 16
Petit Fours, Graduation Cheese 58

DIPS

Asparagus Dip, Hot 17
Broccoli Dip With Crudites, Pat's 20
Caviar Dip 31
Cheddar-Bacon Dip, Hot 26
Chili Dip, Celebration 9
Green Goddess Dip 71
Guacamole Dip 9
Sombrero Dip, Linda's 19
Spinach Dip, Frisco's 39
Taco Dip, Seven Layer 19
Thousand Island Dip 71

EGGS

Deviled Eggs a la Caviar 68
Deviled Eggs, Pigskin 10
Eggs in Aspic, Shimmering 75
Tea Eggs, Kathy's Exotic 63

INDEX

FILLINGS

Apricot Basket Filling 60
Apricot Filling 53
Lime Curd Filling 52
Raspberry Filling 29
Viennese Chocolate Filling 29

FRUITS

Apples, Hot Cheddar-Bacon Dip with
  Sliced 26
Cherries, Singapore Brandied 65
Fruit, Anytime Brandied 72
Fruit Canapes, Sparkling 31
Grapes, Creme de Menthe 39
Persian Melon, Fruit in 34
Pineapple and Cherries, Skewered 36
Strawberries with Chef's Cream Mold 24
Strawberries Romanoff 47

MEATS AND POULTRY

Beef, Pate de Foie Gras Tenderloin of 42
Beef, Tenderloin of 15
Brisket, Gretchen's Barbecued 8
Chicken Balls, Snappy 50
Chicken Liver Pate 15
Chinese Egg Rolls, Pat Ross' 16
Corned Beef Pastries, Aunt Katie's 35
Corned Beef Sandwiches, Jan Head's 46
Drumsticks, Miniature Sesame Almond 39
Ham Balls, Carolyn's 28
Hamburgers, Cathy's Chafing Dish 30
Hamburgers on the Grill, Cupid's Favo-
  rite 66
Ham, Frosted 18
Ham Sandwiches, Emily's Hawaiian 58
Hot Tamales, Ann's Bacon-Wrapped 18
Pork Tenderloins, Cold 22
Pork Tenderloin, Touchdown 68
Sausage Rolls, Binny Webb's Kolbase 46
Stuffed Grape Leaves 74
Tartare Canapes, Opening Night 34
Turkey, Smoked 11

MOLDS AND ASPICS

Caviar-Lover's Mold 28
Cheese Mold, Linda's Ruby 11
Cream Mold, Chef's 24
Fruits of the Sea Mousse 38
Grand Marnier Aspic 31
Shrimp Mold, Super 12
Spinach Mold, Beckwith's Sensational 36
Tuna Mold, Camille's 19
Windy's Wonderful Mold 16

NUTS, PICKLES, CHIPS

Almonds, Wheel of Brie with Glazed 43
Dills, Petite Deli 67
Pecans, Mary Leigh's Spiced 55
Potato Chips, Parmesan Cheese 67
Sherried Dates 20

PASTRIES AND BREADS

Apricot Baskets, Beth's 60
Biscuits with Love Apple Slices, Tiny 55
Brunch Bites, Connie's 38
Caviar Pie, Lake Charles 41
Chocolate Bread 64
Chocolate Forbiddens 40
Corned Beef Pastries, Aunt Katie's 35
Cream Cheese Pastry 43
Cream Cheese Pastry, Mixer 46
Dressing Balls, Vivian Williams' 28
Dynamite Sticks 69
Fillo Pastry, Cinnamon Nut 40
Kiwi Tartletts, Emerald Bay 52
Pecan Pies, Mrs. Williams 59
Pizza, Dot Ward's Mystery 30
Quiches, Black-eyed Pea 43
Quiches, Mary B.'s Miniature Boursin 69
Vanilla Bread 64

SANDWICHES AND CANAPÉS

Appetizer Rubens 72
Asparagus Sandwiches Mimosa 50
Bacon Sandwiches, Mary's 45
Benedictine Sandwiches, Jo Lynn's
  New Orleans 54
Brunch Bites, Connie's 38
Corned Beef Sandwiches, Jan Head's 46
Green Bean Sandwiches, Janie Brister's 55
Hawaiian Sandwiches, Emily's 58
Mushroom Tea Sandwiches, Natchez 51
Pineapple Sandwiches, Honey's Pretty 51

INDEX

Sausage Rolls, Binny Webb's Kolbase 46
Spinach Sandwiches, Grace's 23
Strawberry Sandwiches 57
Tomato Canapes, Tempting 23
Tartare Canapes, Opening Night 34

SAUCES

Avgolemono Sauce 74
Caviar Sauce 33
Hollandaise Sauce, Failure-proof 27
Remoulade Sauce, New Orleans 21
Romanoff Sauce 47
Sweet and Sour Sauce 16
Tenderloin Sauce 22

SEAFOOD

Caviar Dip 31
Caviar-Lover's Mold 28
Caviar Pie, Lake Charles 41
Chinese Egg Rolls, Pat Ross' 16
Crabmeat a la Verner 76
Fruits of the Sea Mousse 38
Lobster, Chafing Dish 35
Lobster Medallions with Caviar Sauce 33
Seafood on Ice 75
Shrimp Biloxi, Marinated 26
Shrimp Chowder, Alabama 66
Shrimp Dijon 76
Shrimp, Golden Isle 62
Shrimp Mold, Super 12
Shrimp Remoulade, New Orleans 21
Tuna Mold, Camille's 19

SPREADS

Asparagus Dip, Hot 17

Artichoke Spread, Chafing Dish 22
Butter, Almond 31
Butter, Bleu Cheese 15
Butter, Chocolate 65
Butter, Drawn 75
Butter, Vanilla 65
Corned Beef Sandwiches, Jan Head's 46
✱ Mayonnaise, Curried 11
Mayonnaise, Food Processor 8
Mustard, Horseradish 9
Mustard, Hot 16
Mustard, Marvelous 18
Pate, Chicken Liver 15
Pate de Foie Gras, Mock 42
Spinach Sandwiches, Grace's 23

VEGETABLES

Artichoke and Lemon Tree 27
Artichoke Heart Flowers 33
Artichoke Hearts Roquefort 76
Artichoke Spread, Chafing Dish 22
Artichokes with Sauce Vinaigrette 42
Asparagus Sandwiches Mimosa 50
Black-eyed Pea Quiches 43
Celery with Leftover Cheese 51
Grape Leaves, Stuffed 74
Green Bean Sandwiches, Janie Brister's 55
✱ Marinated Vegetables, Spicy 12
Potatoes, Caviar 74
Potato Peels with Caviar Dip, Baked 31
Spinach Dip, Frisco's 39
Spinach Mold, Beckwith's Sensational 36
Spinach Sandwiches, Grace's 23
Tartare Canapes, Opening Night 34
Vegetable Salad, Winning 69

"Best of the Best" Cookbook Series:

	ISBN Suffix
Best of the Best from Mississippi $12.95	09-7
Best of the Best from Tennessee $12.95	20-8
Best of the Best from Florida $12.95	16-X
Best of the Best from Louisiana $12.95	13-5
Best of the Best from Kentucky $12.95	27-5
Best of the Best from Alabama $12.95	28-3
Best of the Best from Georgia $14.95	30-5
Best of the Best from Texas $14.95	14-3
Best of the Best from Texas (hardbound) $16.95	34-8

Other Quail Ridge Press Cookbooks:

	ISBN Suffix
The Little Gumbo Book (hardbound) $6.95	17-8
The Little Bean Book (hardbound) $9.95	32-1
Gourmet Camping (hardbound) $10.95	23-2
Hors D'Oeuvres Everybody Loves $5.95	11-9
The Seven Chocolate Sins $5.95	01-1
A Salad A Day $5.95	02-X
Quickies for Singles $5.95	03-8
Twelve Days of Christmas Cookbook $5.95	00-3
Country Mouse Cheese Cookbook $5.95	10-0

ISBN Prefix: 0-937552-
All books are plastic-ring bound unless noted otherwise.
To order by mail send cash, check, money order, or
VISA/MasterCard number with expiration date to:

QUAIL RIDGE PRESS
P. O. Box 123
Brandon, MS 39043

Please add $1.50 postage and handling for first book;
50¢ per additional book. Gift wrap with enclosed card
add $1.00. Mississippi residents add 6% sales tax.

To order by phone: 1-800/343-1583.

Mississippi residents may call collect: 825-2063.
Write or call for free catalog of all QRP books plus a
complete description of all the cookbooks listed above.